UN
LO
CK
ED

Copyright © 2025 by Martijn van Tilborgh

Published by AVAIL

All rights reserved. No portion of this book may be reproduced, stored in a retrieval system, or transmitted in any form or by any means—electronic, mechanical, photocopy, recording, scanning, or other—except for brief quotations in critical reviews or articles, without prior written permission of the author.

Scripture quotations marked NIV are taken from the Holy Bible, New International Version®, NIV®. Copyright © 1973, 1978, 1984, 2011 by Biblica, Inc.™ Used by permission of Zondervan. All rights reserved worldwide. www.zondervan.com. The "NIV" and "New International Version" are trademarks registered in the United States Patent and Trademark Office by Biblica, Inc.™ | Scripture quotations marked NKJV are taken from the New King James Version®. Copyright © 1982 by Thomas Nelson. Used by permission. All rights reserved. | Scripture quotations marked NLT are taken from the Holy Bible, New Living Translation, copyright © 1996, 2004, 2015 by Tyndale House Foundation. Used by permission of Tyndale House Publishers, Inc., Carol Stream, Illinois 60188. All rights reserved.

For foreign and subsidiary rights, contact the author.

Cover design by: Sara Young
Cover photo by: Andrew van Tilborgh

ISBN: 978-1-964794-65-5   1 2 3 4 5 6 7 8 9 10

Printed in the United States of America

UNLOCKED

OPEN YOUR MIND
TO NEW POSSIBILITIES

MARTIJN VAN TILBORGH

*To the countless voices throughout my
journey who have unlocked my mind
with new possibilities and ideas.*

CONTENTS

INTRODUCTION 11

CHAPTER 1. **THE AMBIGUOUS GOD** 15

CHAPTER 2. **BUILD *YOUR* DREAM** 23

CHAPTER 3. **"THE CALL" IS NOT ENOUGH** 31

CHAPTER 4. **THE ADVANTAGE FACTOR** 39

CHAPTER 5. **BRAVING THE EDGE OF CHAOS** 51

CHAPTER 6. **ALWAYS REMEMBER THAT YOU ARE GOD'S SECOND CHOICE!** ... 59

CHAPTER 7. **KILLING MOSES** 69

CHAPTER 8. **LONGING FOR THE WILDERNESS** 79

CHAPTER 9. **THE CHALLENGE OF REAL CHANGE** .. 87

CHAPTER 10. **LIQUID ASSETS** 97

CHAPTER 11. **SUCCESS IS CLOSE AT HAND** 105

CHAPTER 12. **YOU'VE GOT TALENT!** 113

CHAPTER 13. **BUILDING TOWNS WITHOUT WALLS** 121

CHAPTER 14. **FINDING YOUR UVP**............127

CHAPTER 15. **THE DISCOMFORT ZONE**..........137

CHAPTER 16. **THE GREAT ATTENTION SHIFT**......149

CHAPTER 17. **SHEPHERDS IN THE WILDERNESS**...159

CHAPTER 18. **GENERATION NEXT**...............169

INTRODUCTION

Let's face it—most leaders are stuck. They're locked into a system of expired strategies, clinging to outdated formulas that no longer move the needle. Meanwhile, the Church is crying out for something more. Not just more programs, but more impact. Not just more activity, but more transformation. If you're reading this, it's because deep down, you know there's a problem. But more importantly, you know there's a solution—and that solution starts with you.

This book isn't about minor tweaks or surface-level adjustments. It's about stepping into the kind of leadership that turns the world upside down. It's about breaking the mold, disrupting the status quo, and leading the charge into uncharted territory. But here's the hard truth: you can't lead a movement if you're stuck in a system designed to keep you safe.

Think about Moses. He didn't lead by staying in Pharaoh's palace, enjoying the comforts of royalty. He led by walking straight into discomfort, confronting the powers that enslaved his people, and trusting God to do the impossible. Think about David. He didn't lead by wearing Saul's armor. He led by trusting in his

UNLOCKED

God-given uniqueness—a slingshot and five stones—to face a giant no one else dared to challenge. And Esther? She didn't lead by blending in with the crowd. She risked everything to save her people, knowing she was called "for such a time as this."

Their stories are not just ancient history; they're your blueprint for the future. God has always called leaders to step out, stand up, and do what no one else is willing to do. And that same call is on your life.

It isn't easy. It will stretch your faith, test your resolve, and demand everything you've got. You'll have to unlearn the patterns that keep you small and embrace the uncertainty of walking with God into the unknown. But here's the promise: God never calls you to a place He hasn't already prepared for you. The challenges ahead are not barriers; they're stepping stones to the kind of leadership that changes lives and advances His Kingdom.

This book is your guide to unlocking a new kind of leadership— one that opens your mind to new possibilities and challenges you to rethink your preconceived notions of what it looks like to lead well. Through raw reflections and hard-won insights, we'll explore how to let go of expired paradigms, embrace discomfort as a catalyst for growth, and align your leadership with the vision God has for you. We'll confront the lies that hold you back—the temptation to settle, the fear of standing out, and the pull of conformity—and replace them with the truth of who God is and what He's called you to do.

God has placed His Spirit within you. Just as He empowered Moses, David, and Esther, He's empowering you to lead boldly and courageously. The same God who parted the Red Sea, guided Israel through the wilderness, and raised Christ from the dead is working in and through you. This isn't just a call to lead differently—it's a call to lead with power, conviction, and purpose.

Each of these thought-provoking chapters contains expanded, previously written articles designed to challenge and inspire you. Whether you read cover to cover or jump between topics, each chapter offers fresh insights that allow you to focus on the ideas that resonate most with your current leadership journey.

So, what will you do? Will you play it safe, or will you dare to depart from outdated leadership models? The choice is yours but make no mistake: the time to decide is now. Let's get to work!

CHAPTER 1

THE AMBIGUOUS GOD

*Discovering the One Who
Was, Is, and Is to Come!*

After forty years of wandering through the wilderness, Moses encountered God at the burning bush. The last thing on his mind was to return to Egypt, a land associated with deep trauma that he finally managed to lock away. He had thrown away the key a long time ago!

Yet this supernatural encounter would cause him to face his demons and deliver his people from bondage. However, Moses was confused by the whole situation. He had two major questions that needed to be answered before he could embark on his mission:

1. "Who am I?" (Exodus 3:11)
2. "Who are You?" (Exodus 3:13)

Moses was insecure about himself and his ability to get the job done. For starters, he wasn't a great communicator. He hadn't spoken much for the last four decades as he wandered through the wilderness herding sheep. Also, he wasn't too excited about delivering "the word of the Lord" to the man who practically raised him, especially since his message wasn't particularly encouraging.

Though insecure, God assured him he was the right man for the job. He provided Moses with a practical solution for his speech impediment by assigning Aaron, his brother, as his "mouthpiece" and gave him several "tricks" to demonstrate his spiritual authority.

The second question was more challenging to answer. *Who are You? What's Your name?*

On the one hand, Moses couldn't deny that the spiritual experience at that bush was real and transformational. Yet, at the same time, he was unsure about the identity of this god that was sending him on what appeared to be a suicide mission.

He wasn't confident in his ability to accurately articulate who was sending him.

It makes sense when you think about it!

Moses had grown up in environments that would have caused most of us to become spiritually schizophrenic, at best.

For starters, he was raised by three different sets of parents and cultures who each worshiped different gods.

First, there were his natural parents. However, he moved homes before he was old enough to understand who the God of Abraham, Isaac, and Jacob was.

In Pharaoh's house, many gods were worshiped. The most prominent one among them was Ra, the sun god. As a young man, Moses was indoctrinated with the idea that you really wanted to stay on Ra's good side, or else. So, picking a fight with that guy to get his people out wasn't a small ask.

Through a series of unfortunate events, Moses ended up in the desert, where he met Jethro, the priest of Midian, who adopted him into his family. One could argue that Moses ended up "unequally yoked" by marrying the daughter of this strange religious character. I'm not exactly sure what a priest of Midian believes, but it doesn't sound very "Christian."

From the context of his upbringing, the question, "Who do I say sent me?" seemed a fair one to ask. Moses got to know quite a few gods over the years, which made him wonder which one he was talking to.

Now, here's what I'm getting at: The answer God gave Moses regarding His identity was astounding and profound.

God told him in verse 14, "Tell them that I AM WHO I AM has sent you!" (Some translations say, "I'll be who I'll be.")

Wow, it's hard to come up with a more ambiguous answer than that, right?

Really? I am who I am? That's the best You've got? C'mon! You gotta give me more than that!

When you read the complete account of Moses' calling, you'll discover that God didn't fill in the blanks related to defining His identity. The answer remained ambiguous and impractical at best.

He told Moses not to worry too much about the specifics regarding His identity. He would just "be who He would be" as Moses would embark on his assignment.

The only tangible answer God gave Moses was that He assured him He was the same God of his father—the God of Abraham, Isaac, and Jacob (see Exodus 3:6).

> # Although God doesn't change, our perception of who He is constantly changes.

Well, at least he got that out of his burning bush experience. Rest assured, the God his ancestors had worshiped was the same God he had just conversed with.

But what did all this mean? "I am who I am"? It's kind of open-ended, isn't it?

In pondering these questions, here's what I learned:

1. **We're all on a journey.**

Although God doesn't change, our perception of who He is constantly changes. This is true for both us as individuals and humankind as a whole. Throughout history, God has continued to surprise humanity with what appears to be an ongoing process of progressive revelation about the truth and nature of His being.

Consider this remarkable Scripture from Exodus 6:3 (NKJV): "I appeared to Abraham, to Isaac, and to Jacob, as God Almighty, but by My name Lord I was not known to them."

Apparently, God could reveal one aspect of who He was while another part of His identity remained hidden from that generation. In this case, God was known as the all-powerful one, yet by the name "Lord," He wasn't known to them.

God Almighty defined precisely who God was to Abraham.

He was the creator of all things.

Everything belongs to Him.

However, there was more about God that was hidden from him. Years later, some of the "more" was about to be revealed to Moses.

By calling Himself Yahweh ("I am who I am"), God tried to explain to Moses that there was more to be discovered about Him, things hidden from previous generations. Instead of spelling out the "more," Moses was invited on a journey of discovery that, over time, would reveal new things about God that were previously hidden.

Scripture teaches us that God "declares the end from the beginning" (Isaiah 46:10, NKJV), implying that we find ourselves in the middle of that same journey Moses was invited into—a process that pushes us forward into discovering more of who God is.

2. **God will not be defined.**

Throughout history, many well-intended people have tried to define God. Even scripture has been used repeatedly to attempt to decipher and define the anatomy of the Divine.

It makes me think of the following verses: "You search the Scriptures, for in them you think you have eternal life; and these are they which testify of Me. But you are not willing to come to Me that you may have life" (John 5:39-40, NKJV).

Instead of looking at scripture as a means to define God, look at it as inspired text that points us in the right direction, like lamp posts light the way in which we should go—light and direction for a journey of discovery that generations past have started and that we now are privileged to continue.

Don't look at the Bible as the definitive word of God, but rather a word of God—a word that speaks of the unfolding story of the divine dance that God is involved in with creation.

The Bible is too small. There is so much more.

> **Who God is always falls outside our existing paradigms, thus creating that relationship of ambiguity.**

Please don't take my word for it. The Bible teaches us that it only contains a sampling of who God is. The apostle John puts it this way in the last verse of his gospel: "And there are also many other things that Jesus did, which if they were written one by one, I suppose that even the world itself could not contain the books that would be written" (NKJV).

Our world is too small to even begin to define all God is and what He has done, let alone what He will continue to do!

Who God is always falls outside our existing paradigms, thus creating that relationship of ambiguity.

3. **God of the past. God of the present. God of the future.**

In Revelation 4:8 (NKJV), John speaks about "the God who was and is and is to come." This could imply that the nature of God changes throughout time, that the God of the past is different from the God of the future. This couldn't be further from the truth! It's not that God constantly changes His mind constantly; rather, we change our minds about who He is.

The God who was. We can read the stories of how God interacted with the "heroes of old," how He surprised humanity every time with a more extensive understanding of "who He was" through the lives of His people.

He showed Abraham, who was accustomed to a culture where "god" needed to be appeased through sacrifice, that he no longer needed to do this. This was a revolutionary revelation that changed the trajectory of humanity.

He showed Moses a "moral framework" through the Ten Commandments that would revolutionize the culture of the day and would set Israel apart from all the other nations. He showed through the life of Jesus that what was true for the Jewish people was now also true for the whole world!

The God who is. Who God was to the heroes of the Bible has become the foundation of who He is to us today. What surprised the early church in the book of Acts when the Holy Spirit came on the day of Pentecost has become the status quo of our belief system today.

UNLOCKED

The challenge is not to embrace the God who was or even the God who is. The real challenge is to seek the God who is to come! The reality is that the God who is will become the God who was tomorrow. We need to understand that the journey continues.

The God who is to come. Like Moses, God invites us on a journey through which we get to be surprised by new aspects of "the ambiguous God," who is who He is—a journey that will allow us to participate with Him in seeing His Kingdom come to earth as it already is established in heaven! A Kingdom that transforms all of creation through righteousness, peace, and joy!

Yes, God is everything we ever believed He was. Indeed, He is everything we believe He is. Yet, all that doesn't even begin to scratch the surface of who He is to become!

CHAPTER 2
BUILD *YOUR* DREAM

Don't Let Competition Cripple You.

When you want to own the tallest building in the city there are two strategies to accomplish that vision. The first is simply to tear down and demolish every building in town that is taller than yours. This is probably the easiest way to accomplish the desired outcome. The second is to actually build the tallest building.

For some reason, human nature tends to pick the first strategy over the second. We've seen this strategy a lot in political campaigns during election season. Whoever paints the most negative picture of his or her opponent usually wins the election. The problem with this strategy is that making everybody look worse doesn't make you any better. You are still you, exactly the same way you were before you tore the other person apart.

Sure, you may end up with the "tallest building in town," but only at the expense of others and not because your building ended up being any taller than before.

It's a spirit of competition that leads us down this path. A spirit that shouldn't be part of our thinking to begin with. In fact, it may be worth asking whether the desire to build the tallest building is actually rooted in the right mindset.

Could there be an alternative option that will allow you to be successful without having to "beat" someone else?

Throughout the entire New Testament, there is a recurring theme among the disciples. They talk about it a lot. They appear very concerned with the question of who is the greatest among them.

"At that time the disciples came to Jesus, saying, 'Who, then, is greatest in the kingdom of heaven?'" (Matthew 18:1, NIV). This is just one reference that mentions the ongoing conversation on the same topic.

Isn't that interesting? Of all the things they could have been concerned about, the question that seemed to occupy them the most was whether he was greater than the next disciple. We tend to read these stories and shake our heads, not realizing that we're often guilty of that same narrative in our ministries and organizations.

"For I say to you, among those born of women there is not a greater prophet than John the Baptist; but he who is least in the kingdom of God is greater than he" (Luke 7:28, NJKV).

This verse is fascinating to me. It speaks about two paradigms:

1. Those born of women
2. Those who are in the Kingdom of God

Whenever Jesus compares and contrasts these two "worlds" and shows us the difference between them, I like to believe that He wants us to learn something.

In His first example, Jesus speaks about a world or system in which there can be only one who is the greatest. There can be only one winner in this "system." The climate and culture in this environment are one of competition. Everyone is competing for that No. 1 spot. In this example, Jesus had already given that spot to someone called John the Baptist. John was the greatest within that category. Nobody could take his spot. It belonged to John!

Imagine being in an environment like that. That really sucks, right? You put effort and hard work into it, all the while knowing that it's unlikely that you'll ever become the greatest because that spot has already been taken by someone else. You are going to have to settle for either second (or third) place ... at best. Or you could discredit "John" to try to gain the upper hand.

How frustrating!

In this world, John becomes the role model for greatness. Everyone within that worldview strives to become a little bit more like John to compete. Yet all know they will likely never match up to his greatness. They will never even get close. Everyone in that "box" knows they will always be inferior to the one who has already been proclaimed the greatest.

In our ministries, we tend to do exactly the same thing the disciples did. We find the greatest one, model our ministries accordingly, and strive to be as much like the No. 1 as we can be.

We do ourselves (and God) an injustice by thinking like this. This mentality or paradigm creates hierarchy and competition, and it keeps us mediocre.

We focus on how we can earn more points on the scoreboard, not realizing the scoreboard only references how we rank in a world of mediocrity. The best thing that can happen to us within that "paradigm" is that you and I become the best mediocre versions of ourselves that we can possibly become.

If that's the game you want to play, then you should certainly keep doing what you are doing. Who knows, maybe you can do a little better than that person next door.

Personally, I would like to be part of the other world Jesus talks about. That world is much, much bigger. In that world, even the smallest person is bigger than the winner in the other "world."

> **There is no end to the diversity of plans and purposes He has for us.**

A businessman once told me, "If you can't be No. 1 in your category, you need to create a new category for yourself to be No.1 in." Those are some great words! They made me think about God's "categories" for His people.

Ask yourself this question: How many designated categories do you think God has for His people? The answer is so simple, yet so hard for us to understand. His "portfolio" of available categories for us is endless. There is no end to the diversity of plans and purposes He has for us.

By unique, authentic, and divine design, we all are created differently. We all are endowed with gifts that have been given only to us and nobody else. Therefore, I need to play a role in the earth that only I can play. Only I can dominate my designated category because, by definition, nobody else "fits." I am one-of-a-kind!

Again, this is easy to understand and even talk about. It's another thing to actually live it.

God's Kingdom is a world that is created to facilitate extreme diversification. Instead of it being a hierarchy organized vertically, it is horizontally organized through diversification.

It requires a different way of thinking!

Once we grasp it and become who we are supposed to be in His image, we automatically trump the greatest in the inferior carnal world.

Isn't that amazing? I sure think so!

It's actually super logical and simple. Yet, at the same time, we tend to default to modeling ourselves according to ministry templates delivered to us by "the greatest." When we replicate pre-existing categories dictated by others, we miss the target, compare ourselves to others, and are tempted to tear down others who are "greater" than us.

UNLOCKED

Joseph's dreams were a threat to his brothers. Who did he think he was? There was no way they would bow down to their little brother's dream, so they decided to eliminate him. He had become a threat, so he had to be dealt with. Surely, they weren't going to just stand by and watch their brother build the tallest building in their town.

Little did they know that the same God that gave Joseph a dream wanted to give them a dream as well.

You see, the fact that Joseph had big dreams didn't mean that his brothers couldn't have big dreams as well. Their perceived threat was rooted in the same exact wrong mindset that there can only be one "greatest."

In God's Kingdom, everybody can be a winner. No, not in some weird way where "everybody gets a trophy," but yes, God wants to give a BIG dream to all of us.

Let me explain.

I often ask the question, "What happens when God shows up in a place? What happens when His glory manifests?"

When you ask a question like that, you get all kinds of answers. You get answers like this:

- When God shows up the blind will see!
- When God shows up the lame will walk!
- When God shows up people will get saved!
- When God shows up bondage is broken!
- When God shows up even the dead will be raised!

> **As leaders, we merely have to facilitate an environment where God can manifest Himself in our midst!**

Even though all those things are true, there is something far more profound that happens when God shows up. Let's read about it:

> *"And it shall come to pass afterward*
> *That I will pour out My Spirit on all flesh;*
> *Your sons and your daughters shall prophesy,*
> *Your old men shall dream dreams,*
> *Your young men shall see visions" (Joel 2:28, NKJV).*

As ministry leaders we've often been told that somehow we are the ones that need to provide vision for our congregations. This couldn't be farther from the truth, and this verse proves it.

> **Dreams and visions belong to all people, not just a few select ones.**

UNLOCKED

As leaders, we merely have to facilitate an environment where God can manifest Himself in our midst! Why? Because when He does, that old man who had lost his dream a long time ago will dream again. That younger generation that was going nowhere . . . fast . . . will suddenly receive vision!

Dreams and visions belong to all people, not just a few select ones. Collectively we can impact culture and influence change as we manifest our individual dreams in the earth.

When God's vision and dream manifest through someone's life, it makes us bow down.

Why?

Because the manifestation of His dream is the manifestation of His presence. His presence will make every knee bow. It's the nature of God's presence. Throughout the Bible, you see men and women fall on their faces when He shows up. Bowing to someone's dream is bowing to God Himself.

Sure, Joseph's manifested dream compelled his brothers to bow. But I'm convinced that Joseph was prepared to do the same thing to his brothers' dreams if they would have given God the opportunity to give them a dream as well. They had a role to play, too. But because they were blinded by the wrong paradigm, all they could see was Joseph's dream.

Maybe we shouldn't try to build the tallest building in town. Maybe we should stop comparing ourselves to others and simply build the dream that God wants to give us.

Let's dream together so we can change the world together!

CHAPTER 3

"THE CALL" IS NOT ENOUGH

Three Things You Need to Truly Fulfill God's Purpose for Your Life

It was New Year's Eve, 1994. Through a series of seemingly random circumstances, I was a last-minute attendee at Mission 1995, a mega event being held in the convention center in Utrecht, The Netherlands, where I lived.

The speaker that night was from the U.K., and his message was based on Isaiah's calling described in Isaiah 6:8 (NIV, emphasis added): "Then I heard the voice of the Lord saying, "Whom shall I send? And who will go for us?" And I said, *"Here am I. Send me!"*

As I was listening to the message, the words echoed through my spirit over and over again.... "Whom shall I send? Whom shall I send? Whom shall I send?"

Up until that moment I had long had a sense that perhaps the call of God was upon my life. But that night it became clear without a shadow of a doubt that, yes, He was calling me for something that would alter the trajectory of my life forever.

That evening I decided that I was "all in." I put all my eggs in the basket of ministry.

Over the next decade and a half, I wholeheartedly invested my life in what I understood one does when called to the ministry. I preached, got involved in evangelism, led small groups, led a youth group, and planted several churches. I even became a missionary to Africa for three years.

I got involved in pretty much any and every form of "traditional ministry" that one could.

Being part of larger ministries helped me pursue serving God over the years; they oftentimes had so much going on, and they always needed (often volunteer) help to get the job done. Convinced that God had called me, I was always the first one to raise my hand to volunteer for something.

MY "FINDING NEMO" MOMENT

Through a series of unexpected events, things shifted instantly and dramatically as my family and I moved to the United States from Africa within a three-day window. One thing we knew for sure—it was God at work leading us to make this shift. Other than that, we were left with more questions than answers.

When our family of five arrived with only suitcases to start our new lives on the other side of the ocean, I had what I now call my "finding Nemo" moment.

When we arrived in Orlando, Florida, the only people we knew were my in-laws. In fact, we ended up moving into their spare bedrooms for several years.

We had no "ministry" connections. No "home church." Nobody to tell us how to do ministry.

This reminded me of the storyline in the movie *Finding Nemo*,[1] where the tropical fish in the aquarium at the dentist's office are determined to get out, to find a life of meaning beyond the tank, where they exist only for decorative purposes. They come up with all kinds of "projects" to leave the aquarium and get into the ocean, but without success.

Finally, they succeed through a new strategy that clogs up the filter of the aquarium, leading to them temporarily being put in plastic bags. Then they roll out the window into the Sydney harbor, to live the life they were destined for.

In the last scene of the movie, the fish are floating around the harbor in their plastic bags, celebrating and shouting for joy. They finally feel they are living the life they were always supposed to live—not realizing they are still trapped in the bags.

As the celebration fizzles out, it all suddenly gets awkwardly quiet. The fish look at each other from their different bags until one of them nervously poses a question:

---

[1] Andrew Stanton, *Finding Nemo* (May 30, 2003; Burbank, CA: Walt Disney Studios Motion Pictures).

Now what?

Roll the credits.

I knew just how those fish felt. Our move to America had seemed like a release into our next season. God had called us, and now He was sending us to the United States. We were excited until the initial anticipation fizzled out and I asked myself... *Now what?*

In our previous situations there had always been someone else in charge who provided the template of ministry we followed. They created "the schedule" we would follow:

On Sunday you show up and preach.

On Monday you show up and pray.

On Tuesday you do community outreach.

On Wednesday you do small group.

And so on.

Now nobody was telling me what to do and, as a result, I was faced with two options:

1. I was going to have to find a larger ministry I could join that would provide me with a new template to follow.
2. I could give birth to the very thing that God had actually called me to.

The latter seemed to be the right choice but also the most overwhelming one. We chose it, nonetheless.

BEING "CALLED" IS NOT ENOUGH

This decision propelled me forward on a journey that (in hindsight) made me realize that "being called by God" isn't enough.

In fact, there are three things that every person needs to have to live a life of significance—three things that can only be acquired by allowing God to take you on a journey that will elevate your perspective.

Let me explain.

John the Apostle was on the Isle of Patmos in exile when he wrote his revelation. In chapter 4 of the book, he described seeing a door open in heaven: "After this I looked, and there before me was a door standing open in heaven. And the voice I had first heard speaking to me like a trumpet said, 'Come up here, and I will show you what must take place after this'" (Revelation 4:1, NIV).

John was "down there" when God called him "up here."

Being "called" is not enough! You also need to "see."

Sure, "down there," John was able to hear the call of God coming from the door "up there," but he wasn't able to see his future that was visible beyond the door.

In order to see, he had to be elevated to another level. God was calling him higher so John could gain access to three crucial ingredients needed to experience success in life and ministry.

If all you can do is "hear" and not "see," living out what you believe to be the call of God on your life is going to be limited to what you can see "down there."

Being "called" is not enough! You also need to "see."

And in order to see, you need to be elevated as John was. Like John, we need to break away from everything that keeps us "down there." That could include:

- The culture we grew up in.
- The education we received.
- The religious climate that conditions our thinking.
- The way we were raised.

We need to make a conscious decision not to allow ourselves to stay in a place where our environment dictates how we work out the call of God on our lives. Instead, we need to decide to break away from everything that keeps us "down there" so that we can elevate our vantage point and gain access to what is needed for authentic ministry.

> **If clarity of vision is the destination, perspective is the map itself.**

By "coming up here," John gained access to three things pertaining to his future that were needed for him to be effective in his call.

1. Clarity of vision
2. Perspective
3. Direction

Let me elaborate.

Clarity of vision. Think about a map on a GPS system. Your destination or vision needs to be clear for the device to be useful. John's elevated vantage point provided him with clarity of vision, a clear purpose of what he was to accomplish, and a destination.

Perspective. If clarity of vision is the destination, perspective is the map itself. It provides context for your vision. Vision without context is useless. Vision doesn't only need a context; it also requires an understanding of the context in order to be interpreted. Acquiring perspective gives vision a place in the context of everything else. Perspective will allow you to widen your lens to see where your vision fits in with God's bigger plan.

Direction. Direction is the strategic piece of the puzzle. Now that you know where you are going and where you are in the context of that destination, you need to determine your "route." You can determine your direction only once you know where you are going and what the options are for getting there.

UNLOCKED

You have to allow God to detach you from everything in order to get "up here."

Clarity, perspective, and direction are crucial to truly fulfill your calling. Without them, you end up running in circles. You can't acquire all this "down there." You have to allow God to detach you from everything in order to get "up here." With Him.

If you're called by God, I want to encourage you to stop following the ministry templates religion tries to put on you and to answer the call to "come up here" so He can show you things pertaining to your future.

CHAPTER 4
THE ADVANTAGE FACTOR

See Beyond Your Current Reality

The Kingdom of God is BIG.

Very big. In fact, it is so big that seeing only a glimpse of it will disrupt (and likely destroy) any "box" we have built for ourselves. I got one of those glimpses on the night of Easter 2008, a night that changed my life forever and put me on a journey that helped me be delivered from many preconceived ideas I had about church, ministry, life and even God Himself. I was confused, frustrated and, to be honest, annoyed with God. I sort of understood what Jonah was feeling after God grew a plant to provide him shade from the sun—just so He could send a worm to damage the plant and make it wither away (Jonah 4:6-8). I was lying in bed that night asking myself questions: Why would God do this to me? Why would He be so cruel, and why does He have to be such a bully?

I just didn't understand. The ministry I thought I had was gone. It had come quickly, but it seemed to have disappeared even quicker. Three unexpected things had happened. First, the financial crisis of 2008 had hit—and hit hard! During one of my ministry adventures, I had a divine appointment with someone from Iceland who helped fund my ministry. The financial crisis caused Iceland to essentially go bankrupt overnight. Their currency plummeted in a downward spiral to the point where it was worth only a fraction of its original value. This instantly dried up my financial resources, as the monthly support that I got from Iceland ceased.

Second, the ministry I was part of at the time went through some hard stuff. We had been highly committed to this ministry for over a decade; we had moved from continent to continent five times in our commitment to its vision. I don't regret any of it for even one second.

However, a series of events led to a crisis in the ministry that caused it to implode. It shrunk down to just a handful of people. Third, for some reason, certain doors that had been wide open suddenly started closing for no apparent reason. In one instance, a leader within the network I had developed in Vermont created confusion about me among the statewide leaders, which resulted in resistance against my coming back there to minister. I was essentially shut out of the state by the same church leadership who had welcomed me with open arms just a year earlier. To say I was confused is an understatement. Our financial situation had become bad. Really bad! It happened so fast I hadn't even been aware of the seriousness of the situation. I added up all our debt and came to the realization that we owed well over $60,000 to various banks and institutions. Our economic situation back in 2008 wasn't going to provide us with the means to ever pay that kind of money back. I felt like I was on the verge of a breakdown. We had just moved into a new apartment and had no clue how to pay our rent—in addition to all the other bills that had started to pile up quickly.

NOW WHAT . . . ? (HOW ABOUT THE NEW VISION)

I remember lying in bed one night looking at my wife, Amy, in despair and asking her, "Now what?" As soon as I spoke these two simple words, something supernatural happened. Instantly, I was caught up in another realm. I'm not even sure how long I was there, as I had lost all sense of time. In that moment I was struck with what I can only explain as muteness. I couldn't speak. I could identify with what Zacharias must have experienced when the angel took away his speech (Luke 1:20). I started crying, which I really don't do very often. Amy thought I was having a stroke and started to panic. Then I saw a story unfold in my spirit. It was the story of Jesus and His disciples.

For three years they had the time of their lives—I saw it right in front of me. It was almost tangibly visible. It made me wonder, How could life get any better than this for these disciples? They were walking with Jesus and got to learn from Him up close and personal. They were healing the sick. They were raising the dead. They were casting out demons. Every day they got to experience the amazing teaching Jesus was giving to large crowds. They witnessed miracles where multitudes were fed supernaturally and where storms were calmed by the sound of His voice. Wow! That was it—that was purpose. They were experiencing destiny like they never had before, like they never had even dreamed of before. They had reached the ultimate goal and purpose for their lives. They were born to live this life! At least, that's what they thought. Suddenly, one day, their paradigm was disrupted when Jesus sat them down and spoke the following words: "But very truly I tell you, it is for your good that I am going away" (John 16:7a). In other words, He told them the amazing things they were experiencing were going to stop—had to stop. In fact, it would be to their advantage if all of it did stop. In that moment, Jesus introduced them to a reality much bigger than the limited box they had created for themselves. The paradigm they lived in was about to be crushed in order to show them an advantage they couldn't see from where they were at that time. Sure, life was about as good as it gets in their paradigm. But from where God was sitting, there was more. Much, much more!

Their initial reaction was to quickly forget what they just heard Jesus tell them. They didn't want their current experience to stop. What could possibly be better? Then, suddenly, when they were least expecting it, the impossible happened. Jesus actually went away like He had said He would. In a moment's time, they found themselves not in the middle of one of Jesus's incredible ministry adventures but, rather, gathered around a dead body in a tomb where Jesus had been laid to rest. It's funny how our human minds work.

We always tend to default back to what we know based on our past experiences, the way we were raised, the things we were taught, and the culture we grew up in. And that's exactly what the disciples did. They went back to the only thing they knew was "right." They had grown accustomed to the excitement of Jesus's ministry. All they knew how to do was be around Him, wherever He was. And even though He was dead, at least they made Him smell good with all the treatments they were giving Him. I suppose it gave them a false sense of religious accomplishment.

Then, after three days, even that illusion was taken from them. At least within their paradigm it was. They still were failing to see the advantage Jesus had talked with them about—the advantage of His departure! The truth was, Jesus was fully alive and well. They just couldn't see it! Jesus existed outside their current reality, where He was trying to get their attention so He could pull them outside of the limitations they had built for themselves.

As I was watching this story in the trancelike state I was in, something remarkable happened. It was as if my own life story was laid on top of this scenario I was watching unfold right in front of me. On some level, I experienced what the disciples must have experienced as they went through their crisis. Like the disciples, I had come to believe that (what I had defined as) my ministry up until that point was the life I was supposed to live all the way to the end. And like the disciples, I had failed to see the "advantage factor" that existed beyond my current reality.

THE ADVANTAGE FACTOR

As soon as I was able to peek beyond my limitation into a reality I didn't know even existed, I heard the sound of His voice saying: "Everything must die first!" I can still hear those words today as clearly as I heard them then. In that moment I came to the realization that if we truly want to experience the fullness of His resurrection power, we will need to experience death first. You can't be resurrected unless you die first. It's pretty simple, really! In an instant, I was back to "normal" and able to explain to Amy what I had just experienced. I knew what I needed to do next.

> # There's no real point in trying to keep something alive that God has declared dead.

The following day, I literally killed my ministry (or what was left of it), despite people in my life discouraging me from doing so. I knew it had to be done. There's no real point in trying to keep something alive that God has declared dead. Here's the reality. God has an advantage factor for each and every one of us. It's a reality that you can't even dream or imagine. It's something that exists outside of our current paradigm but that He desperately wants to show us. Once I saw this advantage for my life, it took me on a path that deconstructed much of my belief system and much of what I had defined as my ministry. No, it wasn't easy (to say the least). But was it worth it? Absolutely! I'm not saying I have arrived. The journey is far from over. In many ways, it has just begun. There always remains another advantage to be discovered. A new way to look at the same things. A higher perspective. We can train our minds and spirit to pursue these advantages and discover new realities like this on an ongoing basis. Some of these shifts will be small and seemingly insignificant, but others will be life-altering and impact the trajectory of your life.

EXPAND YOUR PARADIGM

Albert Einstein said this: "We cannot solve our problems with the same thinking we used when we created them." Those are profound words. We tend to look for solutions to problems within the context of our current paradigms—problems that wouldn't even be problems if it weren't for the paradigm we are in. I know, I know! This sounds complex. Let me attempt to explain it with a story about something I experienced some years back.

A pastor from a local church invited me for a free breakfast at his church. "A free breakfast?" I asked. "Yes!" he said. "A free breakfast! Bring your wife and we'll have fun. There are a ton of other people coming. You'll enjoy yourself." Of course, I knew there was no such thing as a free breakfast. Someone is going to pay for it somewhere. I somehow had this uncomfortable feeling that even though this was an opportunity that was presented as "free," we would be the ones paying for this breakfast. I was right! Looking back, the best way to explain the whole experience is by calling it a Christian timeshare presentation. It didn't take long for me to figure out what it was really all about: the church wanting to expand into a bigger, better, nicer facility. The breakfast was simply a platform for pitching the new building project. The sales pitch was convincing. Everything the pastor said sounded logical and made perfect sense. The breakfast itself was pretty tasty, which put us all in a good mood. It didn't take long before the first people in the room started reaching for their checkbooks.

It was like a QVC presentation. The lines were open! Yet, while listening to this seemingly flawless pitch, I couldn't help but notice something wasn't sitting well with me. I just couldn't put my finger on it. Besides the fact that I think new building projects for churches are boring and predictable, I knew on a deeper level that something was off. Suddenly, I had an epiphany. It was the paradigm in which the sales pitch was delivered. You see, we structure our ministries according to certain assumptions. One of the arguments the pastor used to support his pitch was this. He said:

> *"Well, my friends, we all know that on Sunday morning, we experienced some amazing growth. We are super thankful to the Lord. As you have noticed, this building we are in has become a little tight. One example is the room next door. It comfortably holds forty children during a Sunday morning service. For the last several weeks, we've been having fifty children in that room. It has become too tight. If we want to have a bigger capacity to minister to more kids, we need to have a bigger facility. I propose to you this new building*

plan. It's going to require $2.6 million to get started on this project. I want to ask you to seek the Lord to find out what you should give."

Now, on the surface that all sounds great, right? You can't argue with him for wanting to minister to more children. I can certainly appreciate his desire to take the ministry to the next level. The problem with the picture is the paradigm in which the pitch was communicated. The paradigm controlled the message (and even the vision) to the point that it reduced it to something that could happen only within a religious, pre-defined set of rules. Think about it! By saying, "We need a bigger building in order to minister to more kids," he was effectively saying that the only way to minister to kids was in that room next door! I'm sure he wasn't the only one looking at the situation under the same set of assumptions. Where do these assumptions come from? Let's say we did spend $2.6 million on that new building. The limitation of forty kids is gone, but now it's replaced by another limitation of, let's say, one hundred kids. There is no businessperson in the world who would invest that kind of money for such a small return. He or she would think, There has to be a better way. And they'd be right!

UNLOCKED

You see, too many times, we tell people how the giant should be defeated.

What would happen if we were somehow able to remove all the assumptions from our thinking and allow our spirits to be in tune with God's Spirit to get new, innovative, creative ideas from Him on how to do ministry outside of our current view of what is possible? In other words, what if we tapped into the advantage factor, a new reality that we were unable to see before? Think about this. What if we were to take a fraction of that $2.6 million and facilitate a platform from which we could equip the church families to minister to kids? Not so much by telling them how to minister but by allowing them to tap into the creative inspiration of the Spirit in order to devise forms of ministry that suit the individual. Not ministry that's done in church on Sunday morning, but ministry done in the community as part of people's everyday lives. The families in our churches are already in contact with the families in the community. Everyone's kids already go to the same sports clubs, schools, birthday parties, and other activities. If we were able to facilitate a platform that would equip people to become effective in the sphere where they already are planted, wouldn't that be more effective than building a bigger building—as well as cheaper and more fulfilling, exciting, and diverse?

You see, too many times, we tell people how the giant should be defeated. We tell them to put on Saul's armor and go forth bearing his heavy sword because that's the way this battle is fought. But what would happen if we instead allowed people to find their sling (whatever that means for them) and face the giant in their faith instead of ours? Then how many giants do you think you would slay on a $2.6 million budget? That's right! There is no limit! Let's enter the advantage factor!

CHAPTER 5

BRAVING THE EDGE OF CHAOS

Why Innovation Is Our Only Option

As leaders we've been told that we need to remove ourselves from the minutiae of the details and position ourselves at 30,000 feet, gaining the vantage point a true leader should have as they look at the world around them. Flying any lower would take away the advantage that the bird's-eye angle brings us as leaders.

I'd like to propose something different.

No, I'm not proposing that we should lose altitude. As a matter of fact, I want you to consider that maybe you are not flying high enough.

You see, the higher you fly, the more you can see and the more context you have.

Sure, you might lose sight of certain details, but the understanding of the bigger context that you gain may outweigh the loss that you'll experience.

I have come to believe that God is calling us even higher as leaders, to gain visibility on things we couldn't see before, to provide us with context crucial to understanding how to position ourselves in our generation.

In Isaiah 46: 9-10 (NIV), God declares something that provides us with insight to gain the ultimate bird's-eye perspective needed to lead effectively!

I am God, and there is none like.
I make known the end from the beginning,
from ancient times, what is still to come.
I say, 'My purpose will stand,
and I will do all that I please.'

As (church) leaders we tend to believe that we as a generation are the center of the universe, and that both the past and future gravitate around us as the epicenter. The world revolves around us.

This is far from the truth.

When God declared "the end from the beginning" and "what is still to come," He wasn't just thinking about us.

God doesn't limit Himself to an isolated segment in time or a generation but rather looks at human history as a whole. In His view, our generation is merely a link in a chain of events that pushes creation to *the end*.

You see, there are things "still to come" for each generation to do. It's each generation's purpose to manifest new things that will bring us closer to the end. It's our responsibility as leaders to recognize what those things are and to lead our generation to manifest those things in the context of who we are and where we are in history.

The Word that has been declared from the beginning pushes creation forward consistently, as an invisible force, into new things that are not yet done. God's spoken word pushes creation forward all the time into new things.

We can't escape it. We must yield to it as leaders! What we will leave behind must be different from what we inherited.

The only way to see who we are supposed to be is to fly higher—higher, not to just see what we are to accomplish in our lifetime, but more importantly, who we are in history and what role we ought to play in manifesting the things declared from the beginning.

Gaining a higher altitude will inevitably provide us with a perspective that will show us both the need as well as a roadmap to innovate in our lifetime rather than maintain (and many times strengthen) the status quo.

Our only option is to innovate!

Once you come to peace with the fact that innovation is our only option, you'll start seeing the concept throughout the Bible over and over again.

Let's break down the word "innovate." According to Webster's dictionary, it means:

1. A new idea, method
2. The introduction of something new

We are called to introduce something new in our generation—something that has never been done before.

Our biggest enemy? The old!

Isaiah says it like this in chapter 43:18-19 (NIV):

Forget the former things;
do not dwell on the past.
See, I am doing a new thing!
Now it springs up; do you not perceive it?
I am making a way in the wilderness
and streams in the wasteland.

The things of the past program our minds, and that's a problem because God always wants to do something new in each generation. The old is often good. Why leave it behind in pursuit of something else?

Innovation requires us to forget those former things and focus on the new thing that God wants to do in our lifetime.

Just because we inherited our world from generations past who innovated in their time doesn't mean we're exempt from the responsibility to innovate ourselves in our generation.

Most leaders agree with the concept of innovation. However, true innovation isn't easy. We often pretend to innovate while in reality we are merely adapting to new circumstances or optimizing within an existing structure. While adaptation and optimization may create the illusion of innovation, we need to understand the difference if we want to be effective as leaders.

ADAPTATION

We saw a lot of this in 2020. Circumstances changed and forced us to do something different, not by choice, but because we can no longer do what we used to do in the past. We simply adapt to what we call the "new normal" to survive in the new climate.

This cannot be confused with true innovation. If anything, adaptation is the same thing we've always done, just a different version of the same thing.

Throughout the coronavirus pandemic, we've seen a lot of churches adapt. They continued to do the same thing they had been doing all along, just an online version of it—the same worship set, the same preaching, the same venue, with nobody in the pews.

Adaptation will never make it into the history books.

Adaptation isn't moving the needle of history forward. Nobody is going to look back one hundred years from now and remember how awesome it was when we preached the same sermons over the internet in front of an empty auditorium.

In the big picture of history, nobody is going to care!

In the big picture of history, it was just another expression of the same thing.

Now, don't get me wrong. Sometimes we have to adapt to circumstances. Being agile enough to do so when the context changes is important to the survival of the organization. However, adaptation will never make it into the history books.

OPTIMIZATION

Where adaptation shifts us horizontally to a different context, optimization pushes us to a level of excellence within an existing context. It has everything to do with improvement within a current position.

In other words, optimization only happens within a context that already exists. Yes, change is required to optimize, but not the type of change that is required to innovate. Change in the context of optimization is vertical. It has everything to do with accomplishing marginal improvement within an existing structure, such as better communication, better software, better programming, better resources, better facilities, and better infrastructure to do what you are currently doing.

> When you stay too long in a God-given season, that season will ultimately enslave you!

Optimization doesn't have to be bad until it becomes bad!

There was a reason God instructed Moses to build a Tabernacle in the wilderness and not a temple. Sure, a temple would have been much nicer than a tent, but it would have kept them from one thing: progress!

When you stay too long in a God-given season, that season will ultimately enslave you! Optimization can do just that. It's great to strive for excellence unless excellence keeps you from moving forward.

God's people were sent to Egypt by divine instruction so that they could escape a famine. It was a true blessing. However, when they established themselves in that God-given place, they "optimized" their lifestyles while Egypt slowly became their limitation, keeping them from moving forward.

Even though optimization can be good, it has the potential to strengthen the status quo while keeping us in bondage to the past.

INNOVATION

Innovation doesn't just happen. It requires courage and true leadership. Innovation happens when we put everything at risk for what has never been done before—something new!

To acquire the type of vision that causes true innovation, we need to fly high—high enough to see the things that are *not yet done,* so that we can make them happen in our generation.

Innovation happens at the edge of chaos!

It happens where developed land stops, and undeveloped land—chaos—starts. It only happens where chaos is cultivated into new opportunities that will advance the Kingdom into places it couldn't get to before.

Remember, the very definition of innovation is "the introduction of something new."

UNLOCKED

The "new" will inevitably disrupt the status quo and will ultimately find a pathway to turn chaos into cultivated land where its environment will flourish.

Don't be deceived. It doesn't stop here. This newly cultivated land can turn into the status quo of tomorrow and potentially keep the next generation from innovating.

However, let's brave the edge of chaos in our time and let's manifest something new that the history books will look back on as remarkable.

Innovation is our only option!

CHAPTER 6

ALWAYS REMEMBER THAT YOU ARE GOD'S SECOND CHOICE!

Your Calling Is for the Benefit of Others, Not Yourself.

I discovered a long time ago the truth of the saying that "information is powerful." If you're a preacher, a motivational speaker, a teacher, or an author—or you have ever listened to or read one who made an impact on you—you've probably already come to that conclusion as well.

Actually, you most likely became who you are today because of that discovery. The right information for the right person at the right time can change their world for the better and forever. It can permanently change the trajectory of our lives. Information can shortcut our learning curve, simply because it offers us a pathway to a desired result that we couldn't see on our own.

UNLOCKED

Now, this is nothing new. Scripture teaches us the power of information throughout. In fact, the very existence of the Bible itself demonstrates the invaluable impact that information can have on people. The word of God, packaged in book form, has made the Kingdom of God accessible to countless people throughout history.

Jesus summed it up when he declared, *"And you shall know the truth, and the truth shall make you free"* (John 8: 32, NKJV).

Knowledge (or the information) of the truth can deliver you from all kinds of "evil" that keep you stuck, in pain, and depressed. "The truth" is sort of a "catch-all" solution for all kinds of suffering we experience as people. It allows you to discover the kind of freedom that the Kingdom of God has to offer—good news for the poor, the brokenhearted, the blind, and the oppressed (see Luke 4:18).

If you're called by God (and if you're breathing, then take that as a given), chances are, He has given you a message—a message so powerful that it can deliver others from the pain they are experiencing in their lives.

Tony Robbins once said that there are only two types of people in the world. First, there are those who run away from pain. The others are those who run toward pleasure. The sad reality is that many people don't really know where they are going in life, but they know one thing.... they don't want to experience the pain that they are feeling! They want to run away from it.

Your message can move people from pain to pleasure. From bondage to freedom.

Other than Jesus, the ultimate "messenger" found in scripture is surely Moses. Think about it: God trusted him with a message that would ultimately deliver a nation from over 400 years of pain and suffering.

> **God has given you a gift that only you possess. In it lies what the business world calls your competitive advantage.**

In studying the life and history of Moses, I have found five things that we should learn as "messengers" and "influencers" to apply to our lives and ministries.

1. You have what it takes.

I picked up my phone one time and on the other end was a very prominent ministry leader. The day before I had spent eight hours with him and his team to create a marketing and communication blueprint to help increase the impact of his message. Some of the dialogue had been centered on identifying and defining just what God had given him uniquely to say.

Over the years I have learned that the only way to be successful as a ministry leader is to clarify what "your lane" is. God has given you a gift that only you possess. In it lies what the business world calls your competitive advantage.

UNLOCKED

When I have conversations like that one while I am coaching leaders, I will try to drill down to the core of someone's existence. This makes such engagements very interesting, but sometimes also very uncomfortable and personal.

In some cases, it will even make someone question themselves. This is exactly what happened in this particular case.

"Do you think I have what it takes to do this?" was the question I was asked.

I answered with a question of my own: *"Did God give you a message?"*

His response was a firm *"YES."*

"Well, then," I said, *"if that's your answer, it's THE evidence that you have what it takes to do this thing!"*

You see, when God gives you a message, gifting, and anointing, He already has a "market" in mind for it. God gave Moses something to say because He had selected an audience that could benefit from that message. Why in the world would God give you something if He didn't have anyone in mind that would need to hear that message?

2. You are God's second choice.

This brings me to the second thing I learned from Moses....

You are God's second choice!

Don't misunderstand me. I am not saying you are less than others. In fact, when it comes to God's desire for us to know Him and the fullness of the life He has to offer, we are all equally his No. 1 choice.

I'm not talking about when He calls us to Himself. I mean when He calls us to do something for Him.

MARTIJN van TILBORGH

God chose the people before he went to look for a messenger!

The fact that Moses was given a message of deliverance to a people in bondage was not because God wanted to give him a powerful ministry. Of course, He wanted Moses to be a successful leader, but at the same time, this wasn't about Moses at all. It was all about the people.

God chose the people before he chose Moses.

In other words, the people in Egypt were God's first choice. When you read Exodus 2 you see the following sequence of events:

The people cried out because of their pain.

- The cry of the people had gone up to God.
- God heard their groaning.
- He remembered his covenant.
- Then He acknowledged them in their pain.

God chose the people before he went to look for a messenger!

The ministry of Moses and the message that God had entrusted him with were merely the result of the process described above.

The people came first. Moses came second.

In that sense, we are all God's second choice. Why, you ask?

Because we all have received a unique gift from God on some level. That gift was not given to serve ourselves. It was given to add value to the people that God had in mind when He gave it to us.

That awareness should keep us humble. Speaking of which...

3. Your message is not just an opportunity.

If I were Moses at the burning bush, I can imagine that my ego would have been stroked. Think about it. The word of the Lord came to him through a supernatural encounter with God Almighty.

It must have been quite the experience.

> When God is giving you a message, it's not about the opportunity that this brings to you.

And through it, Moses received an assignment, a mandate to do some pretty remarkable things. God promised him at that moment to give him a platform and a ministry that he had never had before.

Moses was destined to speak to the masses (and remember, this was without the internet).

Not only did Moses have a supernatural experience and a profound encounter with the word of the Lord, but he also was given the ability to demonstrate some pretty powerful signs as he was sent to confront one of most powerful strongholds in human history. It was quite an amazing opportunity.

But here's the deal. When God is giving you a message, it's not about the opportunity that this brings to you. It's all about the responsibility that comes with the message.

You see, something happens when you ask God to use you. When God answers your prayer it's all about the responsibility that comes with the task. As someone once said, "With great power comes great responsibility."

Such was the case with Moses.

He received "great power," not to give him a great opportunity, but to give him great authority so that he could fulfill a great responsibility.

One could argue that Moses really didn't have a choice. He got what he asked for! And now he was responsible for what he had been given.

4. Your pain is someone else's gain.

For Moses, the pathway to freedom came at an expense. He understood the pain of Egypt. In fact, he grew up as part of the regime that inflicted that pain on God's people. When he discovered that he and his people were part of the problem he took matters into his own hands and tried to bring deliverance within his own strength.

We all know how that went: his fleshly intervention propelled him into a long and painful process that ultimately qualified him to become God's deliverer to his people. Forty years of detoxing took him to the backside of the desert where he finally was assigned his task.

It was a painful journey. Yet it was exactly that process that qualified him to lead the people where he had gone before. You see, escaping Egypt wasn't uncharted territory for Moses. Life outside of Egypt and the freedom he experienced had become normal to him. He knew the desert like the back of his hand.

His journey and his pain become the gain for countless others.

Like Moses, God uses our mourning and turns it into dancing (see Psalm 30:11). Not just dancing for us, but for others.

It makes sense, because, after all, Jesus said, "we testify to what we have seen!" (John 3:11, NIV).

Unless you've experienced something yourself, you can't be a witness to it. "Testifying" of something you haven't seen actually makes you a false witness (and let's just skip what the Bible has to say about being a false witness: it's not good).

Be encouraged that your journey, your experience, your pain ultimately qualifies you to minister to others who have experienced or are experiencing that same pain.

5. Your message is an accelerator.

Your message can speed up others' move into the more that God has for them—it can provide them with the ultimate shortcut to overcoming obstacles in their way.

Moses' experience in the desert opened up an opportunity for others to get through that wilderness region in just a fraction of the time. When you take a close look at a map, you will discover that the people of Israel could have gotten to where God wanted them to be in about eleven days of walking. What ended up taking them forty years could have been accomplished in less than a couple of weeks, even with one or two rest days.

I call that the ultimate shortcut!

You see, what took Moses forty years to learn created a pathway for others to reach the same destination in a fraction of the time, had they listened (actually, 0.0007 percent of the time).

The message that God has given you can shortcut the learning curve for others. They don't have to suffer the same way you suffered. In a sense, you have paid the price for others, a principle of the Kingdom. Jesus is the ultimate example of that.

Because of your journey, others can skip the line!

So, there you have it: Information is powerful! But with great power comes great responsibility. Let's be responsible, courageous, and confident. Confident that we have what it takes to bring freedom to others. Not because we're so important, but because people are waiting for the message God has entrusted us with.

CHAPTER 7
KILLING MOSES

Why Old Leadership Models Have to Die

Most leaders are not opposed to change. In fact, the desire for change is what makes a leader a leader. However, the margin to absorb change is what keeps leaders from actually changing. In other words, the busyness of the day creates a lack of mental capacity to embrace new opportunities that are often hiding in plain sight.

Instead, we tend to spend our time reacting to circumstances to keep our organizations stable in the midst of a changing context. This "default" setting can leave us emotionally, mentally, and even physically bankrupt, resulting in an inability to recognize the need and the opportunity that change can bring.

> # God Himself puts us in situations where our status quo and "safe place" are disrupted.

Change comes at a price. Often a high price. And when circumstances seem to stabilize, our fatigued minds tend to rush back to familiar places in an attempt to "catch our breath." However, it's often in these moments that the benefits of change present themselves to us in unexpected ways.

In fact, I've come to believe that God Himself puts us in situations where our status quo and "safe place" are disrupted for us to see opportunities beyond our current reality. The Bible is loaded with stories of leaders who rose to the occasion in the midst of changing circumstances.

A HIGHER ECHELON OF LEADERSHIP

After disruption or crisis, our environment tends to normalize, and there is a tendency to go back to business as usual simply because that seems to be the road of least resistance. Instead, I want to encourage you to leverage this moment to ascend to a new echelon of leadership. Now is the time to rise up and move forward into the new opportunities that bring us higher as leaders. If we want to benefit from this moment, we'll have to create enough mental margin in our lives to be able to see the opportunities that are right in front of us.

These new opportunities require the type of change that may forever impact the way we lead. In fact, we may be asked to let certain leadership models die in order to fully reap the reward of what's ahead. Moving forward, we simply can't continue to lead the same way—the way we led that got us to where we are today.

To experience new life, something always has to die first. It's a universal principle in scripture that we must understand if we want to lead on that next level.

THE DEATH OF AN ERA

What I've described above is not a new concept. It's something that has repeated itself throughout history. God always pushes creation to advance. His Kingdom is ever-increasing. As a result, there is a frequent demand for change. The death of something that has served its purpose creates the pathway to new life.

The story of Moses provides us with a prophetic picture of what we're going through today. We can extract many principles and ideas from the life (and death) of Moses that provide us leaders with perspective and clarity.

So here we go!

MOSES MY SERVANT IS DEAD

Throughout history, Joshua has inspired many leaders with his courage and accomplishments. As a leader, he could navigate and lead God's people into a place of promise and abundance.

UNLOCKED

I believe that the key to his great achievements is found in something that God declared to him at the offset of his leadership journey in Joshua 1:2 (NIV): "Moses my servant is dead. Now then, you and all these people, get ready to cross the Jordan River."

For Joshua to break through into the opportunities available to him across the Jordan, he had to understand the meaning of something that he was already aware of: the fact that Moses was dead.

Of course, Joshua knew that Moses was dead. Yet God chose to state the obvious in His first instruction to Joshua as he prepared to move into new territory.

Why would God choose to declare something so obvious at the genesis of Joshua's career?

Could it be that Moses had become the epitome of leadership throughout his forty-plus-year career—a career in which he demonstrated success after success to those who followed him?

Let's not forget that it was Moses who showed up in Egypt and confronted Pharaoh with signs and wonders, demanding him to let God's people go.

It was Moses who ascended the mountain and met with God so he could return with fresh revelation to be shared with the people.

It was Moses who was able to lead God's people successfully for forty years in unfavorable circumstances.

Many of us would kill for a resume like that of Moses. He was a model leader everyone looked up to.

Joshua had to accept both Moses' physical death as well as the death of the model of leadership he represented.

Yet Moses had to die for God's people to reach that next echelon. Not just physically, but also mentally. After spending forty years under Moses' leadership, Joshua had to accept both Moses' physical death as well as the death of the model of leadership he represented. It had fulfilled its purpose. "Moses" had become obsolete for the season they were in. The Moses way of thinking had to be removed from Joshua's mind to enter the promises God had for him.

This new season required a whole new way of thinking and leading. Moses could no longer be used as a point of reference for what successful leadership looked like.

If we allow ourselves to step back and create some mental margin to hear what God has to say to us as leaders, we may hear those same words Joshua heard.

Moses my servant is dead!

Whether we like it or not, whatever got us to where we are can't get us to where we are going!

Sooner or later, we've got to align ourselves with the death of the old, even if the old got us to where we are today.

UNLOCKED

PRINCIPLES OF TRANSITION

When we dive a little deeper into the Moses/Joshua transition, we'll discover several keys that will help us unlock the mindsets needed to embrace the same type of change Joshua had to embrace to be successful.

1. **Moses had to be at peace with his death.**

"'Go up into the Abarim Range to Mount Nebo in Moab, across from Jericho. . . . There on the mountain that you have climbed, you will die and be gathered to your people'" (Deuteronomy 32:49-50, NIV).

Remember, Moses was still alive and kicking while they arrived at the river Jordan. Moses could have been stubborn and kept the reigns of his leadership exactly where they had been for the last forty years. Yet God asked him to go up Mount Nebo to die—to voluntarily lay down his position to lead and venture into a place of certain death.

It took effort for Moses to climb Mount Nebo. Nothing about it was easy. He had to choose to die to position Joshua for success.

Moses had to be okay with dying, so he spent the final moments of his life getting to a place that would ultimately kill him.

2. **The people had to be at peace with the new normal.**

It's one thing for us as leaders to embrace the changes needed to get to where we're going. It's another thing for the people we lead to do the same. After Joshua had come to peace with Moses' death, his next priority was to get his people on the same page. As leaders, we have to include the people we lead in the mental shifts we're going through to get them to follow us in the new season.

Joshua 1 communicates an account of Joshua doing this very effectively, resulting in total alignment of the people with the new vision and model of leadership.

"Then they answered Joshua, 'Whatever you have commanded us we will do, and wherever you send us we will go. Just as we fully obeyed Moses, so we will obey you. Only may the Lord your God be with you as he was with Moses'" (Joshua 1:16-17, NIV).

3. There was a reason God buried Moses.

Did you know that God himself buried Moses? You can read about it in Deuteronomy 34:5-6 (NIV): "And Moses the servant of the Lord died there in Moab, as the LORD had said. He buried him in Moab, in the valley opposite Beth Peor, but to this day no one knows where his grave is."

In fact, even today, nobody knows where his grave is. Why is this so important? Well, could it be that if Israel had known where Moses' dead body was, they would have applied their faith to resurrect what God had destined to die?

I believe they would have. For more than forty years, Moses protected them from the dangers of the wilderness. So much so that "Moses" had become their safe place.

By burying Moses in an unknown place, God would keep Israel (and us) from trying to resurrect the old and would push us to apply that faith to the new things He has in store for us.

This would explain why the devil was contending with the archangel Michael regarding the body of Moses, as we see in the book of Jude verse 9 (NIV): "But even the archangel Michael, when he was disputing with the devil about the body of Moses ..."

The devil would love to present us with the body of Moses so we can be distracted by what will no longer serve us in the future.

> The sooner we allow ourselves to come into alignment with the fact that we've come to the end of an era, the faster we'll reap the benefits of what lies ahead.

CONCLUSION

As church leaders, we have arrived at a place where we can no longer deny the obvious. Moses, God's servant, has died. Not only that, even if we try to find his dead body in hopes of resurrecting him, we will be unable to find him. The sooner we allow ourselves to come into alignment with the fact that we've come to the end of an era, the faster we'll reap the benefits of what lies ahead.

So, let's "kill Moses" by encouraging him to climb that mountain. Let's create margin in our lives to fully embrace the level of change needed to move into that next level of command and authority and fully experience what God has in store for us.

CHAPTER 8

LONGING FOR THE WILDERNESS

How the Pursuit of Potential Can Break You

Many of you reading this will recognize what I'm about to say. Being a leader and fulfilling the dream that God has given you is hard. Sure, once you have reached a level of success, people around you may look at you and think, *it must be easy!*

> **More success will require more faith and more responsibility.**

UNLOCKED

I get it. I was there once myself. Looking at the guys "made it." Those who were leading organizations with big budgets where money didn't seem to be an issue and where everything they undertook seemed to be successful. Somehow, I came to believe the lie that once you had arrived at that level it would require less faith or something.

Years later, now that I have become "one of them," I have come to the harsh realization that the opposite is true.

More success will require more faith and more responsibility.

Yes, I know it sounds counterintuitive, but I promise you it's true.

The pursuit of God's potential in your life will demand a greater level of faith with every success you experience.

And here I was, thinking that I only needed faith in the wilderness.

Yet the promised land is where your faith is truly put to the test. So much so that going back to the wilderness seems like an appealing option.

Let me explain.

I've always been intrigued by the story of Abraham—an ordinary man who grew up amid a pagan society in Mesopotamia, a region now known as Iraq.

One could argue that Abraham was an unlikely candidate to be noticed by God. Yet God, in His unwavering desire to make us prosper, God met Abraham in his idolatry to show him a greater reality of what his life could look like.

In Genesis 12: 1-3 (NIV) we read the following account:
> *The LORD had said to Abram, "Go from your country, your people and your father's household to the land I will show*

you. I will make you into a great nation, and I will bless you; I will make your name great, and you will be a blessing. I will bless those who bless you, and whoever curses you I will curse; and all peoples on earth will be blessed through you.'"

God had seen something in Abraham that he couldn't see in himself. Until that moment, Abraham had assumed a life of mediocrity. Yet God's spoken words caused Abraham not just to see his life as it was, but life as it could be. This new reality gave Abraham the courage to uproot his family and embark on a journey that would revolutionize his future.

Like He saw things in Abraham, He sees things in us that we can't see about ourselves. Things that can become a reality, if we have the courage to leave the old behind in pursuit of the land that He will show us.

You see, God will never speak to our mediocre status quo. He will always speak to our potential future.

Just because God speaks to our potential doesn't mean that it's going to be easy.

The dictionary defines potential as "having the capacity to become something in the future."

UNLOCKED

Now, just because you have the capacity doesn't mean that success is guaranteed.

When I was with Bishop Michael Pitts the other day, he said it this way: "Potential is not what I have done, but what I haven't done, but can still do. Potential is not what I have, but what I do not have, but what I still can have. Potential is not who I am, but who I am not, but still can be."

God speaks to our potential. He speaks about the future as it can be if we're willing to take the journey. However, this whole process is not for the faint of heart. Just because God speaks to our potential doesn't mean that it's going to be easy. In fact, when you study Abraham's journey from Ur to the land that God was showing him, you'll find out quickly enough that he wasn't traveling in a straight line.

His journey took all kinds of twists and turns. At times he seemed to be traveling in the opposite direction to where God wanted him to go. On one occasion he even traveled down to Egypt after finally arriving in his Land of Promise. Let's just say that he didn't pick the shortest route on his GPS. To say that Abraham's journey was confusing and difficult would be an understatement.

Abraham's promised land has become a metaphor for us of the potential God speaks over our lives—our lives as they can be, not as they are. But like Abraham, our journey will likely take some twists and turns.

The price of seeing potential manifest is great.

Jesus says it this way: "Again, the Kingdom of heaven is like a merchant looking for fine pearls. When he found one of great value, he went away and sold everything he had and bought it" (Matthew 13:45-46, NIV).

Potential isn't cheap. Once you've seen the reality of what could be, it will require everything to acquire it. And in the process, you'll be tempted to throw in the towel and give up. You'll ask whether all of this is even worth it. You'll start to redefine the memory of your past and tell yourself that life in Mesopotamia was pretty good, after all.

When, many generations later, Abraham's descendants decided to take the journey to their land of promise, they encountered similar dynamics. We all know the stories of the Israelites complaining against Moses about how they wished they had never left Egypt. They mostly complained about the lack of food. What were they going to eat? At least in Egypt, they had something.

Longing for the past while things get tough is pretty normal. I'm sure we've all encountered this irrational desire at times to go back to what we so desperately hated when we were living it.

Longing for Egypt is one thing. Longing for the wilderness is something else!

Let me explain. Like Abraham, you have heard God declare the potential that He sees over your life. It has helped you escape the environment and culture that you grew up in. Now you find yourself in the wilderness trying to transition into what you believe God wants to give you. The wilderness is tough. You wonder if you're even going to survive it. In those moments you long for the "security" of what once was. The place you left behind.

UNLOCKED

But you push through and start seeing the promises of God manifest in your life. You see the potential become a reality right before your eyes, as you possess the land that God has given you.

In that moment the desire for Egypt disappears. It simply isn't there anymore. Yet it is replaced by something else.

The desire for the wilderness!

If you have never experienced your promised land, you will not understand, but I promise you the struggle is real.

Why would anyone desire the wilderness over the promise?

It's a great question, but again, if you haven't experienced the level of success where you truly start seeing your potential become a reality, it probably won't make sense to you.

Yet desiring the wilderness over the promise isn't a new concept. In Numbers 34 we read the account of two and a half tribes who expressed the desire for the wilderness over the promise. In fact, they settled in the wilderness and never got to experience their promised land long term.

What was it about the wilderness that they liked so much?

Here's my conclusion....

Right after you leave Egypt, the wilderness is a scary place. It feels unfamiliar, unpredictable, and dangerous. Yet after being there for a while, it actually becomes familiar to you. It's not so bad after all.

In fact, the wilderness is pretty predictable. It doesn't require much responsibility. All we have to do is follow the leader. Yeah, there isn't much of an abundance, but come early morning there is always food. Weirdly, the wilderness can actually be a pretty comfortable place to live.

As long as you follow the rules, you'll be okay.

In other words, you learn to trust the process. You wake up every morning, and you get to live another day.

Once you cross that river Jordan these dynamics will change completely. The things you could count on in the wilderness are no longer there. No more manna in the morning. No more leader telling you what to do.

In some ways, you are on your own!

Yes, God will still take care of you, but it requires a different kind of faith.

Instead of going through the routines of the wilderness, you are now responsible for making things happen. No more free handouts.

The wilderness was predictable. You knew what was coming. You knew how God was going to take care of you. It was comfortable.

Now that you are experiencing your promised land, it suddenly isn't predictable anymore. Remember, once the Israelites entered the promised land, it required a different strategy for every city they took.

So autopilot wasn't an option anymore. There wasn't a "standard process" they could follow. How they dealt with their victory over Jericho got their butts kicked in Ai.

You had to stay sharp in your promised land for your winning streak to continue.

No assumptions. You are now burdened with the responsibility to lead well because failing to do so may get you (and others) hurt.

The promised land can wear you out. It can burn you out to the point that you start desiring the wilderness. When you have never been in your promised land, you won't understand. Yet those who

UNLOCKED

have will understand the fatigue that can come with what others perceive as easy.

Today I want to encourage you that those feelings are normal. You are not alone.

Yet at the same time, it is foolish to desire Egypt over the wilderness. It's foolish to desire the wilderness over the promise.

I encourage you to press through and not give up. Like the one pearl, the payoff of the promise is worth the investment of losing everything else.

Hang in there. You're going to make it!

Like Abraham, at the end of your life you'll be able to look back with amazement at how much of the spoken potential has actually become a reality. A reality that didn't just impact your life, but the lives of others, as well as generations to come.

Stay strong!

CHAPTER 9

THE CHALLENGE OF REAL CHANGE

To Step into our Bigger Future, We Must Let Go of the Past

You have probably heard it said that if you keep doing what you have always done, you will get what you always got. That should be depressing enough for anyone who believes that God wants more for us, but it's actually worse than that.

Because if you just keep doing what you have always done, you will find after time that it takes more doing to get what you always got. Doing "the right thing" in the wrong season is counterproductive. Many times, keeping on with the things that provided us with past successes will actually push us into a downward spiral of declining results. It's the law of diminishing returns: You have to pedal harder to maintain your speed.

UNLOCKED

So, not only will simply doing what we have always done keep us from the bigger future God has in mind, but over time, it will even prevent us from maintaining what we have in the present.

For the church to become everything God intends, we're going to have to embrace something called "change." Not the kind that doesn't really matter in the big picture, like switching up the color of paint on the walls in your living room or moving the furniture around in your office to create a new look.

Sure, sometimes a freshen-up like that can contribute to a more enjoyable experience and even create a renewed sense of productivity for a time, but it isn't going to make a lasting difference. The kind of change I'm talking about, the kind I believe is needed to realize what is on God's heart, will be disruptive to every way we've always done things.

It will demand a completely new way of thinking. It will force us to abandon past leadership styles, reject past "best practices," and cause us to change our understanding of what it means to be an effective leader.

> **The old tends to precondition our minds to keep us from the new that God wants to do now.**

We will only get to our best future through innovation, not repetition.

A NEW PERSPECTIVE

Now, I am not saying that we reject everything that has gone before. As church leaders, it's our responsibility to honor the past and look back in history to identify defining moments that got us to where we are today. At the same time, the thing about past victories is that ... well ... they are in the past.

We are called to introduce something new in our generation—something that has never been done. The old tends to precondition our minds to keep us from the new that God wants to do now. The old ways were often good. They produced results. So why leave them behind in pursuit of something else, something uncertain and unproven?

Because the old is our biggest obstacle. Consider what God said through His prophet in Isaiah 43:18-19 (NIV): "Forget the former things; do not dwell on the past. See, I am doing a new thing! Now it springs up; do you not perceive it? I am making a way in the wilderness and streams in the wasteland."

To get a glimpse of the new God is speaking about, we're going to need to look at things from a different perspective.

As church leaders, we tend to believe that we as a generation are the center of the universe, that both the past and future center on what we are doing. The world revolves around us. However, this is far from the truth! When God declared "the end from the beginning" and "what is still to come," He wasn't just thinking about us.

God doesn't limit Himself to an isolated segment in time, a generation. Rather, He looks at human history as a whole. In His view, our generation is merely a link in a chain of events that pushes creation to *the end*.

You see, there are things "still to come" for each generation to do. It's each generation's purpose to manifest new things that will bring us closer to the ultimate end. And it's our responsibility as leaders to recognize what those things are and to lead our people into them.

A COMING CONFLICT

We are not the first to find ourselves at such a moment. Think of when David returned home from leading Saul's army to victory over the Philistines. In 1 Samuel 18:7 (NKJV), we read that the women came out with their tambourines, singing, "Saul has slain his thousands, and David his ten thousands."

It was at this moment that something happened. Something that couldn't be reversed. Angered by the attention given to David, Saul "eyed David from that day forward" (v. 9). The women's song became the catalyst of a conflict. A war that would linger for a long time, but would evidently be won by David.

We are in a place that we have never questioned before because it was something that had always been there.

He was destined not to perpetuate the Kingdom that had been built under Saul, but to establish something that had never been done. In fact, the vision that burned inside the heart of David would ultimately erase all that Saul had built over the forty years of his rule as king.

I believe that the church finds herself in a similar situation today. We are in a place that we have never questioned before because it was something that had always been there. We grew up in it. It defined us. It was part of us. We were part of it.

Yet maybe you have become uncomfortable with it. Unsatisfied with where we are. You can't quite put a finger on it, but it is there. A sense of unease, that there must be something more. Something better. Something greater that God has in store for His people. Something bigger and better for you and me.

If this is you, know that you are not alone. God has awakened a generation destined for greatness beyond what you've ever seen or experienced. A people who will not settle for second best. A people who, despite unlikely circumstances, will choose to believe God and push forward into something that may go down in the history books as one of the biggest church schisms we've ever experienced.

It's Saul and David in the twenty-first century. They are prophetic pictures of the church. They represent mindsets, leadership styles, and models that provide revelatory insight into the state of the church. The church of today as well as the church as she could be—and as she needs to be—tomorrow.

A COURAGEOUS CHOICE

Even though he was anointed king by Samuel, Saul never became one "after God's own heart" as David did when he came to the throne years later. In fact, Saul's kingship was the result of the Israelites' carnal desire to have a king "like all the other nations" (1 Samuel 8:20, NIV).

In other words, God's people demanded a leadership structure that was modeled after the ways of the world around them, rather than something unique. It's a mindset that continues to this day, with churches looking to the world for models of how to do things. So, we have "Christian" versions of what works there, from movies and music to organizations and management.

After he was made king, Saul ruled for forty years, but he wasn't God's first choice. He was the result of a man-made decision that God tolerated rather than initiated. Saul was the choice of the people—and he is an example of how this thing called "freedom of choice" can get us into trouble.

Now, think about the impact of growing up in such a leadership climate. You will simply start embracing the culture and environment because you don't know any better. If Saul is the only leader you have ever known, what point of reference do you have to long for something better?

When I look at the church today, I believe we've done well under the circumstances. However, I have also come to the realization that a lot of what we see today, and a lot of what we've accomplished, has been "under Saul." A lot of our victories and achievements are the results of initiatives modeled after "other nations."

As you decide what side you're on in this looming conflict between Saul and David, it's important to remember one thing. Neither of them is the actual people we encounter in our lives and ministry. We're not fighting against flesh and blood, as Ephesians 6 reminds us.

Having grown up "under Saul," we're actually all Jonathans. Born as Saul's natural son and raised in the palace, Jonathan was conditioned to think and act like an heir and to follow in his father's footsteps as his eventual successor.

> **Do we stay loyal to the establishment we grew up in, or are we going to make a covenant with what God has declared will be in the future?**

However, as Jonathan was exposed to David, he soon realized that perpetuating Saul's government wasn't in God's interest, nor in the interest of the people. He even recognized that the future of Israel was with David as king, not his father.

Like Jonathan, we are caught between two options, each of which asks for our allegiance. Do we stay loyal to the establishment we grew up in, or are we going to make a covenant with what God has declared will be in the future? It is a dilemma.

Even though he declared his loyalty to David, the tragedy of Jonathan's life is that he eventually died in battle with the Philistines, while serving his father Saul, as 1 Samuel 31 records.

The struggle is real: the religious draw to stay part of the old is strong. As Jonathan's story demonstrates, even those who have recognized God's prophetic destiny can be pulled back into the past. The old can put a spell on us.

We must find the courage to break free from the spell of the old and pledge allegiance to the "side" that is destined to win.

ESCAPE THE WILDERNESS WAY

Leadership expert Stephen Covey put it this way: "Each of us tends to think we see things as they are, that we are objective. But this is not the case. We see the world, not as it is, but as we are—or, as we are conditioned to see it."[2]

---

[2] Stephen Covey, 7 *Habit of Highly Effective People: Powerful Lessons in Personal Change* (New York, NY: Free Press, 2004), 14.

None of us is exempt from this. We all see the world as we are conditioned to see it by our culture, our history, our upbringing, our experiences, the media, people's opinions and so on.

As a result, our leadership capacity is limited to the areas where perception and truth overlap. We need to open ourselves to alternative realities beyond our current ones so that our perception of the world around us can be aligned by "truth" in order to lead more effectively.

But it's not that easy. Remember when ten of the twelve spies sent to check out the Promised Land came back with a "bad report," saying that if the Israelites crossed the Jordan, they were all going to die because of the giants there.

Because the people embraced that negative account, God decided to keep them in the wilderness for an additional forty years where those who were twenty years of age or older were destined to die. He told them: "And your sons shall be shepherds in the wilderness forty years" (Numbers 14:33, NKJV).

A MISSED INHERITANCE

By circumstance, not by choice, a whole generation was forced to become something they were never supposed to be. Everything they did for four decades was the result of something they had no control over. The way they acted, the way they thought, and the way their behavior was conditioned were the result of choices another generation made for them.

Instead of becoming landowners in the land of promise, they ended up herding sheep in the wilderness. They had no choice. It was the only way to survive their current situation.

UNLOCKED

What do you think happens when you are forced to become something you were never supposed to be for an extended period of time? You simply start believing that the life you live is the one God intended for you, while in reality there is a whole different world waiting for you beyond the Jordan. You see being a shepherd in the wilderness as the "call" and "destiny" that God has for you.

Could it be that in the same way we, the church, have become "shepherds in the wilderness" today because we inherited a position that God never intended for us to occupy? Our main goal is to strive to become the best shepherd possible!

And yet, by doing so, we're actually strengthening our position in the wilderness.

Perhaps we need to reprogram our thinking, to be aligned with the promise that lies across the Jordan.

CHAPTER 10
LIQUID ASSETS

*Living Water Is Not
Meant to Be Bottled.*

What is the shape of water? Well, it depends, doesn't it? The shape of water is controlled by the shape and size of the container that it is poured into. For example, when water is poured into a glass, the shape of that water takes on the shape of the glass in which it now resides. In fact, it is scientifically impossible for water to take on any other shape than the shape of its container.

Yet water has the unique property to seep into any crack and corner of a space if we were to allow it to do what it does naturally. When we let water do whatever it wants, it has an incredible ability to touch places that can't be touched by anything else.

Water is a metaphor used throughout the Bible to represent the greatest asset that God has entrusted us to bring life to the world around us. There are more than one hundred scriptures that talk about the "living water" that God gives to us as believers. This living water can reach every corner of society if we allow it to do what it does best rather than put it into a shape that limits it from reaching the corners of the earth.

Could it be that we as church leaders have created systems and structures in our ministries that have become a container that limits the shape of water, so it can only exist within the shape of our organizations?

Could it be that we have turned our greatest asset (living water) into a non-liquid asset, keeping it from being exchanged in the open market? In the business world, both liquid as well as non-liquid assets can have tremendous value. However, the full value of a non-liquid asset is not accessible in the present if we want to use it *now*.

Some of the cities in our country that have the highest number of churches per capita seem to struggle the most with poverty, crime, and violence. Somehow, our greatest asset isn't liquid enough to seep into the cracks of society and fix our most basic problems.

As I have considered these issues, I have concluded that we often limit the shape of the living water we've been entrusted with to the four walls of our ministries simply because of wrong assumptions we've adopted as truth. We've been called to reshape water and "liquidize" this asset so that we can truly touch culture and impact our society. To do so, we have to unlearn some basic "truths" that keep us from being effective as the church.

Three basic concepts have helped me become a more liquid leader. I want to share these ideas with you in hopes that they will help you reshape water in the same way it helped me.

MARTIJN van TILBORGH

CORRECT THE TENDENCY TO SEPARATE

In the New Testament, many of the stories Jesus shared were intended to correct our misperceptions and the bad tendencies we might have that need to be corrected. For example, in Matthew 13 we read the well-known story of the wheat and the tares. The danger of passages like this is that because we know them so well, we assume we've learned all we can learn. One area that this parable addresses is the tendency to separate ourselves from the world around us.

> **Instead of trying to separate and isolate ourselves from the tares, we need to allow ourselves to grow where we are planted.**

Verses 24-30 (author emphasis, NIV) says this:

Jesus told them another parable: "The kingdom of heaven is like a man who sowed good seed in his field. But while everyone was sleeping, his enemy came and sowed weeds among the wheat, and went away. When the wheat sprouted and formed heads, then the weeds also appeared. The owner's servants came to him and said, 'Sir, didn't you sow good seed in your field? Where then did the weeds come from?' 'An enemy did this,' he replied. **The servants asked him, 'Do you want us to go and pull them up?'** *'No,' he answered, 'because while you are pulling the weeds, you may uproot the wheat with them.* **Let both grow together until the harvest.** *At that time I will tell the harvesters: First collect the weeds and tie them in bundles to be burned; then gather the wheat and bring it into my barn.'"*

The servants of the man in the story (us) tended to separate the tares from the wheat that were both sown in the same field. Jesus later explains that "the field is the world" (v. 38). Guess what? To reach the world, we have to be *in* the world. And guess what else? There are going to be "tares" growing among us. Instead of trying to separate and isolate ourselves from the tares, we need to allow ourselves to grow where we are planted. Let both grow together until there is a harvest!

This brings me to the second point.

THE GOSPEL TRAVELS THROUGH TRADE

As a kid, I always liked to look at those big maps that tracked the Apostle Paul's travels as he preached the gospel in all corners of the earth. Each journey of Paul's was identified by a dotted line that stretched from country to country and city to city.

It wasn't until many years later that I realized that these dotted lines were not the same dotted lines that one would see if they were trying to pick their favorite cruise vacation on a travel website. These dotted lines were, in fact, trade routes. Paul didn't join a group of tourists on a big recreational boat. He boarded merchant ships that took him from point A to point B.

The truth is that the gospel has always traveled through trade.

Trade happens in every sphere and segment of society. By allowing trade to become the infrastructure and distribution model for the gospel, we will be able to reach every corner of our communities organically. Understanding this causes us to rethink the way we lead our churches.

> **Yet, most of our efforts are geared toward initiatives that strengthen the status quo and that keep our greatest asset non-liquid.**

The truth is that 98 percent of all people in church are not working for the church. Most Christians have jobs in the marketplace. When I say marketplace, I'm not referring only to traditional business. I'm talking about every form of trade that creates culture, including sports, arts, entertainment, politics, education, and much more. As church leaders, we need to learn to leverage the fact that our people are already living and working "in all the corners of the earth." By allowing them to grow where they are planted, we will reshape water to reach those corners until we see a harvest.

Yet, most of our efforts are geared toward initiatives that strengthen the status quo and that keep our greatest asset non-liquid. We don't need another new program or project to reach the world. All we need to do is tear down the walls that limit the shape of water and allow it to flow into places where it experiences the least resistance.

BUILD TOWNS WITHOUT WALLS

In Zechariah 2, we read a story about a man with a measuring line in his hand who was on his way to build Jerusalem. This man reminds me of us as leaders as we attempt to build our organizations and ministries. The man was halted by an angel who questioned his efforts, and the man explained his good intentions to build the city of God.

As the angel and the man exchanged words, it was made clear to the man that he had assumptions that would have kept God's city from developing the way God had intended it to grow. The angel told him that Jerusalem would be inhabited as towns *without* walls and that the Lord would be a wall of fire around them.

This came as a shock to the man. A town without walls cannot be measured! What God wants to build cannot be measured. The man quickly became aware that the very tool he was using to build the city was in fact completely useless in the context of the picture the angel just painted for him.

A measuring line is a tool that references a standard created by man. How many of the standards that we use to measure our work are merely assumptions that keep us from building the right thing? Let's do away with the measuring lines in our thinking and build towns without walls. Let's allow God to be a wall of fire around them. In other words, wherever the church is planted in society, that's where God's wall will be.

The city of God is fluid. It's liquid. It reaches into every corner of society, and it shapes our culture. Let's be liquid leaders and help reshape water in our lifetime!

CHAPTER 11

SUCCESS IS CLOSE AT HAND

The Answer to Your Biggest Challenge Could Be Laying within Reach

I remember it as if it were yesterday. One day back in 2008, I sat down with my wife, Amy, to add up our credit card debt. We knew we had accumulated consumer debt over a period of time, but for some reason, we had never made an inventory of exactly how much money we really owed.

I'm sure the underlying reason was "denial"; I simply didn't want to face the reality of our situation because the truth was too hard to face.

That day I discovered that we owed over $60,000—an amount that was impossible to pay back based on our then-income. I broke out in a cold sweat. I was about to have a panic attack. The reality of our situation paralyzed me mentally as I saw no way out.

But then, in the middle of my despair, I realized something. The same truth that got me spiraling down could set me free. The choice was mine! Was I going to let the reality of my situation control me, or was I going to allow the truth to set me free?

Needless to say, I choose the latter.

As soon as I made the mental decision to allow the truth to deliver me from my despair, I was reminded of the story in 2 Kings 4 about a widow who found herself and her family in a desperate situation. Like me, her circumstances had led her down a path where she accumulated a tremendous amount of debt. There simply wasn't a way out for her unless God intervened. And he did!

The answer for her situation came through a simple question from Elisha: *"Tell me, what do you have in your house?"* (v. 2, NIV). The question asked by the prophet implies that, even in the most desperate situations, there is something close at hand that is the answer to your problem. Elisha's question pushed her to identify the very thing that would become the vehicle of her deliverance.

It was a small jar of olive oil, something seemingly insignificant that became a weapon of war that would lead her to victory, favor, and incredible abundance.

SOURCE OF ABUNDANCE

My main takeaway from this story was that the answer to her problem was not found externally. Her situation was "fixed" through something she already possessed. Something seemingly small didn't just become the antidote to her problems, it became a source of abundance that would leave a legacy for her family.

> **The bridge between lack and abundance is found in something you already possess, not something outside of your reach!**

In my case, the "oil" that I was able to identify was that I had once read a book on Photoshop. That's right, Photoshop, that software that allows you to design stuff.

I must have been very bored, but at one point I had picked up a how-to book from the bookstore about Photoshop and actually read it cover to cover.

That "oil," which appeared to be totally insignificant, would become the source of the abundance I experience today. It allowed me to build seven companies that generate millions of dollars every year.

Here's what I learned from all that: The bridge between lack and abundance is found in something you already possess, not something outside of your reach!

The key is to hear "the voice of God" in your current circumstance that will allow you to leverage something you have already got to take you from lack to abundance. The kingdom of God is always within a hand's reach. The answer to your problem is always already in your possession.

It's all about what you do with what you have already got that will make the difference.

Let me give you another illustration that will show you that the gateway to your abundance already exists where you are. In John 21 we read the story of Jesus's disciples fishing all night and catching nothing. The time, effort, and patience put into their work amounted to zip. The lack they were experiencing was disheartening. That was, until they allowed Jesus to speak into their situation.

In verse 6 (NKJV) we read: *"And He said to them, 'Cast the net on the right side of the boat, and you will find some.' So they cast, and now they were not able to draw it in because of the multitude of fish."*

The voice of Jesus in their situation was instantly able to pave the way from lack to exceedingly abundant.

But what's important to understand is that the answer to their problem was already in their possession. The voice of Jesus was merely putting their mind in the right place to tap into the abundance that already existed in their current situation.

So often we default to looking for answers outside of our situation. But God wants us to leverage what we already have. It's all about what you do with what you have already got that will make the difference.

> # You have something that can be leveraged to get started, even if it isn't ideal.

Here's what I mean. This is how the disciples leveraged what they already had to experience abundance.

1. They used the equipment they already had.

I can imagine throughout the night that Peter and Thomas were having conversations about their fishing equipment.... their boat was getting old. It couldn't compete anymore with other boats that were much better equipped to catch fish. They probably needed to invest in the latest technology that would allow them to be more effective in their efforts. But how would they afford such equipment?

But none of that mattered. The same equipment that was used to catch nothing, was the same equipment that brought in the multitude of fish.

UNLOCKED

Your computer may be old. Your vehicle may not be the best. Just know that you have something that can be leveraged to get started, even if it isn't ideal.

2. They leveraged their current location.

A logical conclusion could have been that they were fishing in the wrong lake. Maybe they (and others) had gone out too often to catch too many fish so that there weren't any left in the lake. They should just get their trailer and drive their boat to another lake.

None of that, either. The same location that brought them lack became the location that got them almost too much to handle.

Just because you live in a small town with fewer opportunities doesn't mean you have to move to the big city to make it. Allow God to speak into your current location to align your mind with the opportunity that already exists within the "lake" that you're fishing in.

3. They didn't look for new partnerships.

"If only I could be on *Shark Tank* and partner with Mark Cuban. Or if only Oprah Winfrey could endorse our product."

It would have been easy for the disciples to dream about some pie-in-the-sky partnership that would probably never happen as being the solution to their problem.

But no, they simply worked with the relationships that were already in place. There was no need to "sell a percentage of the company" to a third party. They simply worked the relationships they already had to get from lack to abundance.

4. They used the education they already had.

Sure, it's always good to learn and develop yourself. However, the disciples weren't exclusively dependent on additional education to be able to experience abundance. They didn't quit their jobs to start a four-year degree in hopes they would catch more after they graduated.

No online course. They simply leveraged the skill and knowledge that was already in place to experience all that God had for them.

The bridge between lack and abundance is not found externally but is right where you are at. All we have to do is to allow God to identify what we should do with what we already have.

This isn't to say that as we multiply our God-given talents we shouldn't invest in better equipment or move into larger markets. The point is that we have what we need to be delivered from our problems if we can discern what it is we need within what we already possess.

Let's stop looking at those who have five talents while we may only have one, saying, "If only I had five, my life would be different." No matter how small or insignificant your "oil" seems to you, it holds the seed of your harvest.

CHAPTER 12
YOU'VE GOT TALENT!

Use Your Gift to Serve Others and Get Rich—in More Ways than One

There are many things in this world that could be defined as "evil." Hate, war, crime, racism, abuse—the list could go on and on. However, one of the most destructive evils I have witnessed in my lifetime is poverty. Webster's dictionary defines poverty thus: "The state of one who lacks a usual or socially acceptable amount of money or material possessions."

Many say that money can be the root of all kinds of evil. But by the same token, poverty can be the root of all kinds of evil, too. A lack of resources can make people do things that under normal circumstances they would never do. Much of the crime we face today in our society is rooted in poverty.

> **The biggest tragedy happens when poverty causes someone to settle for something that is second (or third) best.**

Yet the biggest tragedy happens when poverty causes someone to settle for something that is second (or third) best. Whenever we experience lack, the temptation arises to trade our life for something that could potentially compensate for the deficit we're dealing with. Suddenly we settle for jobs we hate.

Before long, we spend our days doing things we don't want to do simply because it helps us bridge the gap between what we have and what we need to survive. When this happens it becomes increasingly more difficult to break from what keeps you from living a life you love.

Welcome to the rat race!

EXPERTISE AND CURRENCY

There are only a few things more painful than to watch someone give up on their life's dreams and waste their life on doing things they despise, simply to make ends meet. Thankfully God himself declares in Isaiah 61:1 that he brings good news to the poor. His gospel carries some exciting news to those who encounter these dynamics.

What could that good news possibly be?

Well, it's that God wants you to experience:
- A life you love.
- A life of significance.
- A life that adds value to others.
- A life that impacts the world around you.

And you can even make money while you're at it!

No, this is not wishful thinking. In fact, it's God's heart to help us break free from poverty and unleash us into a life of abundance. Not just so that we can be blessed, but so that we can be a blessing to others.

Sure, we're all born into different circumstances in this world. Ours may determine how we start our lives, but it doesn't have to define how we end our lives. Because it's not about what you've got. It's all about what you do with what you've got!

Let me explain. You're probably familiar with the parable of the talents that Jesus told in Matthew 25:14-29, in which a master entrusted his wealth in differing amounts to three servants.

One got five talents, one got two, and one received just a single talent.

You could say that that's not fair, and I get that. However, it's not so much about what you got when you came into this world as it is about what you do with what you've been given.

We don't all come into the world in the same package. Yet, if we're responsible with what we've been given, and we steward it well, we'll be able to reap the fruit of the multiplication that good stewardship brings.

UNLOCKED

Here's the reality. Everyone has been given at least one talent. Maybe yours is very small compared to those around you. Don't be discouraged. That small talent you possess holds the keys to break free from the imprisonment of poverty. It has the potential to grow and propel you forward into a life of abundance and prosperity.

The dictionary defines the word "talent" in two different ways:

1. natural aptitude or skill—"he possesses more talent than any other player"; synonyms are aptitude, gift, knack, expertise.
2. a former weight and unit of currency, used especially by the ancient Romans and Greeks.
3. In other words, a talent is both a "gift/expertise" as well as a financial "currency." Someone's gift (or talent) is directly tied to their financial situation. As someone's talent multiplies, so does the money.

The key is to work within the grace of your talent.

FAITHFUL AND PERSISTENT

When God gives you a gift and you work it for the sake of others, your financial situation will benefit in direct proportion to the increase of your talent. The problem is that, many times, we're not working within the grace of our given talent. We work hard, but impact few. We toil and sweat but live a life of lack.

The key is to work within the grace of your talent. When you do this, your impact increases as well as your finances. You cannot steward your talent without benefiting financially. Financial abundance is the byproduct of stewarding the gift that God has given you.

If you feel like you're stuck in a cycle that seems impossible to break free from, consider the following. Regardless of your social status, race, upbringing, or even the political climate you're in, you've been given a talent by God himself. This talent is your gateway into living the life you've always wanted to live. A life that allows you to turn your passion into profits while impacting the world around you.

No, this doesn't mean that the journey will be easy. In fact, expect some turbulence along the way. But what I can promise you is that God will be faithful through it all. His plan and purpose for your life will ultimately prevail as you remain faithful and persistent through the process.

Here are some practical tips to get started:

1. **Be aware of what you've got!**

That dream that's deep down within your heart. That desire that feels like it's no longer there. That skill or talent that others recognize in you. The thing that has been given to you by God himself. Own it and put it to work with confidence so he can multiply it.

2. **Don't despise the day of small beginnings.**

What you've got may be small, but don't underestimate the power of multiplication. Results are compounded when something is multiplied over and over again. Even the smallest number multiplied over and over again can add up to something astronomical in a relatively short period of time.

3. **Hustle every day.**

You have to work it! Nothing happens automatically. Put the gift that God has given you to work. Not just sporadically, but every day. Maybe you still need that day job (at least for now). But start putting that gift to work in your spare time. Add value to others. Do what you're good at because God has given you that ability to start developing a business out of your passion.

4. **Always add value to others first.**

The Bible says that when you give, it shall come back to you. According to Luke 6:38 (NIV), "Give, and it will be given to you. A good measure, pressed down, shaken together and running over, will be poured into your lap." To experience that type of abundance, we have to give to others first.

Add value to others first. You can never go wrong with that. When you do that, I promise you, God will come through for you so you can live the most fulfilling life you could ever live.

> In fact, you owe the world something. Something precious. Something valuable.

Author and speaker Les Brown said this:

The graveyard is the richest place on earth, because it is here that you will find all the hopes and dreams that were never fulfilled, the books that were never written, the songs that were never sung, the inventions that were never shared, the cures that were never discovered, all because someone was too afraid to take that first step, keep with the problem, or determined to carry out their dream.[3] Don't allow the graveyard to be richer. Instead, let's live life to the fullest.

The world around you doesn't owe you anything. In fact, you owe the world something. Something precious. Something valuable. The gift, the talent that you've been given. Love what you do. Do what you're good at. Add value to the world around you as you put that gift to work and prosper while you're at it.

---

[3] Les Brown, "The graveyard is the richest place on earth.... determined to carry out their dream," *Goodreads*, https://www.goodreads.com/quotes/884712-the-graveyard-is-the-richest-place-on-earth-because-it#:~:text=The%20graveyard%20is%20the%20richest%20place%20on%20earth%2C%20because%20it,someone%20was%20too%20afraid%20to.

CHAPTER 13

BUILDING TOWNS WITHOUT WALLS

Why God Won't Be Measured

In the second chapter of Zechariah, we encounter a man with a measuring line. This man is on his way to the city of Jerusalem, the city of God. He is passionate, full of zeal to help build this incredible city. He wanted to do the right thing and contribute to the strength and effectiveness of what will become a place of refuge for so many people:

> *Then I looked up, and there before me was a man with a measuring line in his hand. I asked, "Where are you going?" He answered me, "To measure Jerusalem, to find out how wide and how long it is." While the angel who was speaking to me was leaving, another angel came to meet him and said to him: "Run, tell that young man, Jerusalem will be a city without walls because of the great*

UNLOCKED

number of people and animals in it. And I myself will be a wall of fire around it,' declares the LORD, 'and I will be its glory within.'"—Zechariah 2:1-5 (NIV)

One thing I know for sure is that this man's heart was in the right place. He loved the Lord, he was excited about the city of God, Jerusalem, and he was committed to giving his contribution to the building of that city so it could serve the community within.

There seems to be nothing wrong with this picture, right?

Just another day at the office for this man, happy to be about the work of the Lord, building the city of God. Many of us are like this man. We're excited about and committed to the work of the ministry (or, at least, what we have defined as our ministry). We want to build "the city of God," His church, His Kingdom.

Our hearts are in the right place, and we can't wait to see this "city" completed, so it can become a blessing to the countless people who will inhabit it.

However, could it be that there was more going on beneath the surface? Could there be a cause for concern? The answer seems to be affirmative when an angel appeared on the scene and abruptly stopped the man from what he was doing.

As this man stopped in his tracks, the angel said in effect: "What do you think you're doing? Don't you know that Jerusalem shall be inhabited as towns without walls?"

The angel made the man aware of something very important. Something he hadn't considered before. Something that would be so disruptive that it would change everything in relation to the activity the man was planning to be involved in.

The man was given a piece of information, an epiphany that would change the trajectory of his "ministry" once and for all.

The angel pointed out to the man that Jerusalem, the city he was measuring and helping to build, wasn't going to have any walls.

What!?

That was a game-changing revelation!

Everything the man had done in his life, and everything he was planning to do, had been based on the assumption that the city he was helping to build was going to have walls. His whole ministry had been founded on that particular assumption.

In fact, he had given his life for this thing!

What would a city without walls even look like? The mere idea of a city without walls seemed to be ridiculous. The walls he intended to build were supposed to be a foundational and defining aspect of the city he sought to develop.

Yet, meanwhile, God had never intended for Jerusalem to have walls.

A sudden awareness came to the man by supernatural intervention that changed his perspective forever.

Remember, the primary tool this man had brought to help him do his work was a measuring line. In fact, he had specialized in using it. For years he had been an apprentice in learning how to use this tool. Through trial and error, he had become an expert at using it. Not only had he become an authority in the field of measuring stuff, he had become an experienced architect who designed blueprints for building walled cities, only to find out that the city he was trying to build was not going to have any walls whatsoever.

UNLOCKED

The very thing he had become excellent in had become irrelevant in the context of this new information. He somehow had to unlearn the very thing he had studied for all his life!

How do you measure a city without walls?

What would it even look like?

How do you even plan to build a city without that structure? Basically, you don't. Yet, God wants a wall-less city. God was making this man aware that what He is envisioning for the city is immeasurable!

God said to him: "Hey! Don't you know? I cannot be measured, and neither can the city that I'm building." He continued to explain to the man that this city would have a multitude of people in it and that He Himself would be a wall of fire around them.

In other words, wherever the people are, that's where the wall will be. Not because we build it, but because God Himself will be it.

Amazing right?

Think about this for a moment: What is a "measuring line"?

Well, a measuring line is a tool that references a standard that once was created by man.

Not by God, but by man.

Somebody at some point in history decided that a foot was a foot. Where I'm from, the Netherlands, we use the metric system. We have meters. The thing about meters is that, at some point, someone (probably Mr. Meter?) decided that a meter was a meter. He set the standard right then and there.

From that point onward, anything that ever had to be measured was measured by that standard. Every measuring line created since has referenced that man's standard.

Could it be that God is trying to remove the measuring lines by which we measure our work?

Could it be that God's standards don't equal our standards?

Could it be that we have measuring lines in our minds that reference a standard that was not meant to be a standard to begin with?

Could it be that we are working on assumptions that need to be challenged?

Could it be that God is trying to remove the measuring lines by which we measure our work?

God's Kingdom is fluid. It doesn't have walls. It flows with its people. Wherever they are is where His city is.

So many times, we have "strategic ministry" meetings to plan how we will grow what we are doing, and we set parameters for what it is going to look like. Yet God says, "I cannot be measured." You cannot design a wall-less city. In God's city, each person is supposed to give birth to a uniquely unexpected expression of who God is. It cannot be measured. It cannot be planned. Like the man with the measuring line, we need to be made aware of this, so we will cease putting effort into strengthening something that was never supposed to be built.

The bottom line: God's Kingdom is fluid. It doesn't have walls. It flows with its people. Wherever they are is where His city is.

An interesting concept, right?

But it's the very opposite of how we traditionally do church. We build walls and point at what's inside of them, we give it a name, stick a logo on the building and call it church.

God's city, His Kingdom, doesn't have walls. It's connected by blood. It's a family of people who collectively, through their efforts, administrate and establish God's Kingdom on earth.

Are we willing to look in the mirror and confront some of the same things the man from this story was confronted with?

Could it be that we have it all wrong?

Is it possible that what we've been building is in fact foreign to God's divine design?

Should we consider the possibility that what we've been training for isn't conducive to the big picture?

Are we willing to consider that maybe God is sending His angels to disrupt our ministries?

Asking for a friend.

CHAPTER 14

FINDING YOUR UVP

Don't Be a Copycat! To Make an Impact, You Must Know What Sets You Apart—Your Unique Value Proposition

Everything starts with identifying your message. What is the unique value proposition God has given you? What value does your calling bring to those around you? This may sound simple, but many I have worked with struggle to answer these questions.

Jesus knew who he was. He knew the specific value he brought to his target audience.

We need to start with identity and purpose. Knowing who you are in Christ is fundamental if you want to make a difference in the world. Even top-level influencers find it hard to identify specifically what they have to offer. Sure, most of them know how to give a generic answer, but this question needs to be answered with precision. What sets you apart from everyone else?

Jesus knew who he was. He knew the specific value he brought to his target audience. When he went into the synagogue at Nazareth, he read from the book of Isaiah:

The Spirit of the Lord is upon me, because he has anointed me to preach the gospel to the poor; he has sent me to heal the brokenhearted, to proclaim liberty to the captives and recovery of sight to the blind, to set at liberty those who are oppressed; to proclaim the acceptable year of the Lord.
—*Luke 4:18-19 (NKJV)*

Isn't that amazing? Jesus didn't come with a generic, one-size-fits-all message. He knew who He was, and He spoke with confidence about what He had to offer to specific people. His message was not abstract. It was practical and clear, tailored to His target audience. Four things stand out about Him:

- He knew He was anointed and called by God with a specific gift; He was able to confidently proclaim who He was.
- He understood His message and its specific value proposition, as He brought good news—healing, liberty, and sight.
- He knew His target audience, the ones who would most benefit from the value He was offering. He knew they were the poor, the brokenhearted, the captives, the blind and the oppressed.
- His message was clear. For instance, one of His target audiences was the blind. What was His value proposition to them? You don't have to be blind anymore! Another target demographic was the poor. His value proposition to them? You don't have to be poor anymore!

Jesus was specific in who He was, who He was trying to reach, and how He was going to help them solve their problems. What is your unique message and gift in your ministry or business or area of influence? What is the value you have to offer? Who are the people who will most benefit from your message? To whom are you sent? It's all about knowing who you are and articulating it in a way that helps the people you're called to reach.

UNITY DOESN'T MEAN UNIFORMITY

God chose to give each and every person a measure of his value to steward. God's distribution strategy is to use us, His body. There are so many sides to God's creative expression that it's impossible for one human to display them. In fact, collectively as humanity, we still aren't able to define the boundaries of His creative expression: He does more than what we can even think or imagine.

The devil will make you believe uniformity is a virtue, but it isn't.

In our limited mindsets, we tend to create ministry templates that allow God to work through us in a limited set of rules we create for Him. Those parameters that we've defined make up only a sliver of the potential spectrum of possibility within God's reality. Yet when we look at our churches, ministries, projects, and events, they all seem to look the same. Why is this?

It's because we fail to see our unique value proposition. We model after each other instead of trying to figure out who God says we are individually. The devil will make you believe uniformity is a virtue, but it isn't.

I discovered this truth several years ago when I was teaching at a Bible college in Aruba, a small island in the Caribbean with one major town where most of the 110,000 population lives. During my week there, the churches organized a March for Jesus through the main streets. They had decided it would be a great statement of unity to march around the city, holding banners and singing songs about Jesus.

I remember standing by the side of the road as hundreds of people marched through the streets. They all wore red T-shirts, sang the same songs, marched to the same beat, and carried the same smiles on their faces. I guess their goal was to show the love of Jesus through these efforts, in hopes that others would be attracted to this display of "happiness and joy."

Now, I have no doubt that these people marched with a pure heart and an upright motivation. Yet, something was terribly off as I watched. It seemed so forced. Fake. It felt like it lacked authenticity. Their walking, singing, and smiling a certain way appeared to have the opposite effect of what they were trying to accomplish. The random bystander on the street was not attracted by their behavior. In fact, they seemed uncomfortable and often looked away in hopes that nobody would hand them one of those balloons or tracts they were carrying.

Suddenly, it hit me. God is not looking for uniformity! He's looking for diversity. Instead of trying to have us all do the same thing, He wants us all to start doing something different!

This was a real eye-opener for me. For so long, I was taught that true unity was created through uniformity. At that moment in Aruba, I started to see the difference between the two. I realized that the opposite is true. True unity is not accomplished through uniformity; it is accomplished through diversity. But diversity will only manifest fully if each of us finds our lane.

PURSUE INNOVATION, NOT OPTIMIZATION

So, let me ask you again: What is your gift? What is your message? What is your unique value proposition? What is your lane? Who are you called to be? Who are you called to?

In Joel 2:7-8 (NKJV) we read how "They run like mighty men, they climb the wall like men of war; every one marches in formation, and they do not break ranks. They do not push one another; every one marches in his own column." This describes the army of the Lord the way it is intended to be. No one breaks rank. Nobody pushes one another. Everyone is in his or her own lane, doing their own unique thing, without competing. And in doing so, they are one.

Unity is the result of each individual finding their own place within the army. No rank is the same. No position is equal. It's uniquely designed for each individual to march. And as we march in that unique, authentic way, we become one.

We don't tend to promote this in our ministries and churches. More often than not, we operate in wineskins, structures, and leadership models that don't facilitate the kind of environment where such identification can take place.

In fact, most influencers model their strategy after other successful influencers—especially in the church and ministry world. This isn't a bad thing; however, innovation is essential if we're going to differentiate ourselves. God is an innovator. When He speaks, He creates things that have never been created. His desire is to do something new, not something that has already been done.

How do I know that? In Isaiah 43:18-19 (NKJV) he says: "Do not remember the former things, nor consider the things of old. Behold, I will do a new thing, now it shall spring forth; shall you not know it? I will even make a road in the wilderness and rivers in the desert."

God declares through Isaiah that He will do something new. But to see that new things spring forth we have to forget "the former things" because they keep us from innovating. It's easy to look at past successes of other people and model what we do after them. That's not innovation. We call that optimization.

When we read scriptures like the one in Isaiah, we tend to mystify the "new thing" God is about to do. We think of it as something intangible—unknowable. In reality, it's far simpler. If we truly believe we're created uniquely by divine design, all we have to do is become exactly who God created us to be. Then, by God's definition, we are innovators.

If nobody is exactly like me, and I become who God intends me to be, I'm bringing something new to the table. I'm bringing something that nobody, past or future, has brought or will ever bring to the table. God does a new thing through us when we become who He created us to be. It's as simple as that.

For decades, athletes from all over the world tried to optimize their high jump skills to increase their results. They used the barrel-roll technique as their default method. Then, in 1968, Dick Fosbury innovated the sport when he introduced the Fosbury Flop, which literally took the sport to new heights. Dick Fosbury tapped into something unique—something that hadn't been done.

As believers, we're called to do the same—to lead—not to follow others' trends. If we truly believe God created us to be unique, there must be something we can do that's never been done before in exactly the same way.

Being aware of the process of innovation is incredibly important. While optimization is powerful and beneficial, it's not going to set us apart. Optimization breeds competition; innovation destroys competition.

Optimization focuses on things like:
- Better technology.
- Better copywriting.
- Better branding.
- Better web design.
- Better customer service and so on.

ONE OF A KIND, NOT SECOND-BEST

Innovation challenges the very framework in which existing things are executed, to create an entirely new framework. Jesus talked about this in Luke 7:28 (NKJV): "For I say to you, among those born of women there is not a greater prophet than John the Baptist; but he who is least in the Kingdom of God is greater than he."

This verse is fascinating to me! It speaks about two paradigms: Those born of women and those in the Kingdom of God. Jesus contrasts these two "worlds" and shows us the difference between them.

In his first example, He speaks about a system in which there can be only one who is the greatest. The culture in this environment is one of competition. John is already the greatest within that category. No one can usurp that No. 1 position. Imagine being in an environment like that. You put in effort and hard work, all the while knowing you can never become the greatest. You'll have to settle for second place at best. How discouraging!

Yet in our ministries and churches, we tend to do exactly the same thing the disciples did. We find the greatest one and model our ministries accordingly. We look at the latest big names and make their ministry model the ultimate goal for our ministry. We think, *If I can do half as well as them, then I'll be doing great.*

We do injustice to ourselves (and God) by thinking like this. It is so shallow. This mentality creates hierarchy and ungodly competition. It keeps us mediocre. We focus on earning more points on the scoreboard, not realizing that the scoreboard we're looking at is referencing how we rank in a world of mediocrity. The best thing that can happen to us within that "system" is that we become the best mediocre versions of ourselves that we can be.

Personally, I would like to be part of the other world Jesus discusses: the world of the Kingdom. This world is much, much bigger. In this world, even the smallest person is bigger than the winner in the other world.

By unique, authentic, divine design we all are created differently. We are endowed with gifts that have been given to us and nobody else. Therefore, I need to play a role in the earth that only I can play. Only I can dominate my category, because, by definition, nobody else fits my category. I am one of a kind!

As long as we try to model ourselves after others, we will miss the mark.

God's Kingdom is created to facilitate extreme diversification. Instead of being a vertical hierarchy, it is organized horizontally. This model requires a different way of thinking. Once we become who we are supposed to be in His image, we automatically trump the greatest winners in the inferior carnal world. Isn't that amazing? It's actually simple. Yet, at the same time, we tend to default back to modeling ourselves according to templates delivered to us by "the greatest."

As long as we try to model ourselves after others, we will miss the mark.

CHAPTER 15

THE DISCOMFORT ZONE

And Why You Should Stay There

What if the very idea of a "comfort zone" is the greatest adversary of growth? What if the safety zone, the tried-and-true business strategies and the rinse-and-repeat formulas that have brought you some success are actually the enemy of your future? The truth is no one will remember the things you did that worked. They will remember what you did that no one else would do. What would it take for you to be an audacious dreamer, undeterred by the risk of an enormous vision? I want to issue a challenge to awaken the disruptive leader within you, the one who finds solace—and maybe even a thrill—in the wilderness of challenge and change. It's easy to lose the heart of what it means to lead with conviction, yet the answer is what drives all revolutionary leaders: Leadership is a continuous pursuit of the extraordinary in the face of the ordinary. It is a lifestyle of healthy rebellion against the status quo, an obstinate pursuit of "different" and an unmalleable expectation to stand out from the crowd and make waves that will change the world. But there are pitfalls and shortcuts along the way—appeals to settle for business as usual. In this article, I want to explore four of the temptations that will derail your journey to becoming an unorthodox leader.

COMPLACENCY: THE WILDERNESS IS NOT YOUR COMFORT ZONE

Many dream about becoming an influential leader—to change the world. Then, when you become a leader … reality sets in. The truth is that fulfilling the dream God has given you is hard. Once you have reached a level of success, people around you may look at you and think, *You have it so easy!* Have you ever heard that before? I get it. I was there once myself, marveling at the guys who "made it." Those who were leading organizations with big budgets where money didn't seem to be an issue and where everything they undertook seemed to be successful. Somehow, I came to believe the lie that once you become one of "those guys," you don't need as much faith to remain successful. In my mind, I would no longer be chasing after the dream. I would just announce my arrival by reclining, kicking my feet up, sipping on my coffee, and eating bonbons.

Fast-forward, and now I have come to be one of "those guys" and have come to the harsh realization that eating bonbons means saying goodbye to success. More success will require more faith and more responsibility. Yes, I know it sounds counterintuitive, but I promise you—it's true. The pursuit of God's potential in your life will demand a greater level of faith with every success you experience. And here I was, thinking I only needed faith in the wilderness! Yet, the promised land is where your faith is truly put to the test, so much so that going back to the wilderness seems like an appealing option.

Sure, right after you leave Egypt, the wilderness is a scary place. It feels unfamiliar, unpredictable, and dangerous. Yet, after being there for a while, it actually becomes familiar to you. It's not so bad after all. In fact, the wilderness becomes not only familiar but attractive. Predictable even! That's because familiarity demands less responsibility. All we have to do is follow the leader. True, there isn't much abundance to go around but come early morning, there is always food. Before you know it, you have made a home in a place that looks and feels comfy but is actually stuffy and even hostile. Don't be fooled! Once you cross that River Jordan, these dynamics change instantly. The things you could count on in the wilderness are no longer there. Said another way—you are on your own! Or so it feels. God will still take care of you, but it requires a different kind of faith. Going on autopilot isn't an option anymore. There isn't a standard process we can follow. The strategy that gives us victory over Jericho kicks our butts in Ai. You have to stay sharp in your promised land in order for your winning streak to continue. You are now burdened with the responsibility to lead well because failing to do so may get you (and others) hurt. The promised land can wear you out and burn you out to the point where you will begin to desire the wilderness.

This is difficult to comprehend if you have not yet made it to your promised land. Talk to any promised land resident, and they will tell you that fatigue is plentiful there. Yet, others won't see it because they will be too focused on being you—that guy. Today, I want to encourage you that fatigue is expected. In fact, if you are fatigued, you are doing something right. You are leading well. Most importantly, you are not alone. Press on, push through it and whatever you do, do not give up. It's not called the promised land for nothing. In fact, there are two promises waiting for you: the promise of pressure and the promise of plenty. Embrace the pressure and reap plenty.

CONFORMITY: COLOR OUTSIDE THE LINES

There's a place for structure, boundaries, and parameters in our business, ministry, and even our families. They give you guardrails, they offer a sense of order when things feel a bit blurry, and, in some ways, they can even protect us. But just like with anything else in life, you must be able to discern the difference between the protective qualities of a framework and the restrictive qualities of rules that keep you small. You only need to look to children to understand the difference.

You've likely seen a child in their own little world, crayons in hand, coloring their little hearts out. Before children develop fine motor skills, they cannot stay within the lines. The shape or figure had order, defined parametric lines—before they got their hands on it! Yet, children are about the most innovative creatures in existence!

So, when I reference lines and colors, I'm talking about the defaults and templates that exist in our business and ministry worlds. There are certain procedures and patterns for how things are done. The catch is that, sometimes, these patterns actually hold us back from innovating. When I was younger, I believed I was called into the ministry. I also believed, based on the ministry templates I'd been surrounded with my entire life, that this limited me to three branches of employment: a pastor, a missionary or an itinerant speaker. Today, I believe God is far more creative than that! When we go beyond our self-imposed limits, we'll find that there's so much more in store for us than the templates we've created for ourselves. You have a unique gift—a unique color. Nobody else in all of history will possess the exact value and color you bring to the table. Therefore, your color automatically falls outside the lines anybody else can draw for you. There is only one you!

What does this mean? It means you're free to defy the expectations and limitations that culture or business models try to place on you. This isn't an anti-authority message—it's an anti-conformity message. So often, our greatest potential lies dormant because we subscribe to the notion that we need to mold ourselves into what's expected of us. When we kneel to expectations, we become a clone of others who kneel to those same expectations. You've got more in you. Coloring outside the lines means we embrace this truth: No one structure can facilitate a world where every individual finds and maximizes his or her unique purpose. This is my call to you today: Get a little messy, break some culturally imposed rules, and color outside the lines!

COPYING: IMITATION DOES NOT EQUAL RELEVANCE

I love this scripture from Ephesians 3:10: "... to the intent that now the manifold wisdom of God might be made known by the church to the principalities and powers in the heavenly places" (NKJV). God is not one-dimensional. He is manifold. By divine design, He's created each individual to display and manifest an authentic aspect of who He is to the world. Our organizations should be unique, creative expressions of who He is so the world around us can get to know Him.

> Instead of staying relevant by copying someone else's ideas, God wants us to create relevance—to set the standard.

Yet so many times, we are merely copy-cats of others: We choose the easy route by finding someone else who has a measure of success, and then we model our organization after them in an attempt to attain greatness. We look at big organizations and try to become like them. I know it's tempting to copy ideas, models, and approaches based on established success stories. I'm sure you have heard the maxim, "Find success by doing what successful people do." While there's some truth and wisdom in this (leaders should always remain lifelong learners), we cross over into the danger zone when we become them. It's the fallacy of remaining relevant. Instead of staying relevant by copying someone else's ideas, God wants us to *create* relevance—to set the standard. He wants us to become an expression of His divine inspiration, which, by definition, is unique and one-of-a-kind. Ephesians 3:10 says the principalities and powers need to be confronted by the infinite spectrum of diverse creative expressions that display who He is. And He wants to do that through you and me! Stop looking for "the next big thing" by modeling after others. Don't borrow from other people. Those things produce mediocrity at best because they were never meant for you in the first place.

Think about the men and women of the Bible whom God chose to free nations, reconcile them to Himself, and invite all of humankind to share in the glory of His Son. Their victories were found in the unique giftings God gave them. Moses was chosen to lead the Israelites out of slavery and into the Promised Land. David was chosen because of his lifelong vocation as a shepherd and warrior—the perfect choice for a king (and a forerunner to Jesus). Paul was charged to be the apostle sent by Jesus Christ. I think you get the picture. We are the body of Christ. This means that our callings are different. They are meant to complement each other—a feat that would be impossible if you were the same body part as someone else. Today, seek inspiration for new and creative ideas—ones that will truly make a difference. You will be surprised at what you find on the other side. Be someone who will make known yet another aspect of His manifold wisdom that has never been seen before!

COMPETITION: WHY BUILD THE TALLEST BUILDING IN TOWN?

When you want to own the tallest building in the city, there are two strategies to accomplish that vision. The first is simply to tear down and demolish every building in town that is taller than yours. This is probably the easiest way to accomplish the desired outcome. The second is to actually build the tallest building. The problem with the first strategy is that tearing down everybody else doesn't actually make you any better. You are still you, exactly the same way you were before you tore apart the other person. Sure, you may end up with the tallest building in town, but only at the expense of others and not because your building ended up being any taller than before. You simply brought others down to your level of mediocrity.

> **The moment you are lured in by the spirit of competition is the moment you put yourself at risk of eating from their table instead of the table God has prepared for you.**

It's a spirit of competition that leads us down this path. A spirit that shouldn't be part of our thinking to begin with. In fact, it may be worth asking the question of whether or not the desire to build the tallest building is actually rooted in the right mindset. Could there be an alternative option that will allow you to be successful without having to "beat" someone else? So often, we tend to focus on how we can earn more points on the scoreboard, not realizing the scoreboard we're looking at is referencing how we rank in a world of mediocrity. The best thing that can happen to us within that paradigm is that you and I become the best mediocre versions of ourselves that we can possibly become. If that's the game you want to play, then you should certainly keep doing what you are doing. Who knows, maybe you can do a little better than that person next door.

There's another option—and, in my opinion, a much better option. One that will not only enable you to build the sky-scraper you dream of building but will also allow you to recruit others who are doing better than you. That's right, your competition can become your collaborators. If you've got other builders on your side, your building will grow much taller than you could have built on your own. So, you start by refusing to operate in a world of mediocrity. You set yourself apart the way God already has. Competition creates an illusion of success. Let's be honest. Business owners hustling and measuring themselves against other successful business owners put off an air of higher-level competency, and ambitious leaders are drawn to that. But you have to be really careful to see through that because the moment you are lured in by the spirit of competition is the moment you put yourself at risk of eating from their table instead of the table God has prepared for you. Make no mistake: You are a one-of-a-kind builder. The value you bring knows no competition.

FROM CONVENTIONAL TO UNORTHODOX

"Conventional" must be eliminated from our business vernacular. It no longer has a place in the vocabulary of anyone who wishes to walk ahead of the pack. Convention, in a sense, is the assassin of impact. To be conventional is to follow the map; to be unorthodox is to draw your own. To be conventional is to use a key to unlock a door; to be unorthodox is to pick the lock. To be conventional is to whisper, "This is what has always worked"; to be unorthodox is to declare, "There's a better way."

Throw out your predictable programs and step into the arena of unorthodox leadership. God uses singular (and unlikely!) voices to capture the attention of an entire nation and, sometimes, the world. There are countless people waiting to hear from those who speak louder than the rest, who are so unorthodox in their thinking that they know—without a doubt—that it is God's maverick spirit working in them and through them simply because of their shameless unorthodoxy.

I don't know if you've noticed, but God is pretty unorthodox. A leader who is humble and courageous enough to allow God to fashion him into His unorthodox image will spread the gospel faster than leaders who choose the path most traveled simply because they are leading the way Christ leads His people. Your unique imprint in God's kingdom will spread like wildfire, and people will notice.

They will know there is something different about you. Like a moth to the flame, they too will begin to brave the Wild West, following your lead, creating a ministry of their own that will shake the very foundations of "acceptable.

Faith grows in tandem with pressure. Leaders can find strange comfort in the constant stretching of their capacity. The way you lead your organization or ministry should be a magnet for souls who are stuck in the same narrative and the mundane rhythms of work. The way you lead should be a crucible of divine challenge that becomes your battle cry, one that doesn't just tickle the ears but marks the heart for eternal purposes.

CHAPTER 16

THE GREAT ATTENTION SHIFT

*Disruption, Innovation and
How Leaders Respond to
a Changing Context*

Not too long ago I sat down with a pastor of a megachurch on the West Coast. He had flown me out to pick my brain about some marketing-related projects for his church and ministry. We were having dinner at a small restaurant in downtown of the quaint California town where he had been a pastor for some time now.

We had a great time getting to know each other while enjoying some incredible food. Halfway through our conversation, he made a statement followed by a question that I have become very familiar with while working with many great leaders over the years: "Even the most committed families in my church only show up 1.8 times every month."

"Wow, that must really be frustrating for you when you preach your six-week sermon series," I remember responding. "How are people going to be fully benefiting from your series if they only hear the first and the fourth while missing out on the rest?"

I knew that making him feel the pain of his reality would cause him to think a little deeper about the real issue and its possible solution.

The truth is that most (if not all) churches these days are dealing with the same dynamic. Ministries all over the country are struggling to get people back in the pews week after week. It's a trend that ministries big and small experience.

My pastor friend then asked me the following question: "How can you help me to get my people to show up every single week?"

I quickly told him that I could not help him solve his problem. Sure, there are tons of gimmicky and manipulative marketing tricks that can be deployed to shame and guilt people back in their seats every Sunday. But is this really what we want to do?

Shifts in attention make previous distribution models obsolete.

The tragedy is not so much that this is an overall trend among churches, but more so that we don't seem to understand what's behind this trend: a great attention shift.

This is not something new. Attention shifts happen all the time. Not just in church, but in every industry and market, we experience waves of change as the attention of the people we're trying to reach shifts.

Shifts in attention make previous distribution models obsolete. We used to buy toys in stores, now we buy them online. We used to go to restaurants for the convenience of not having to cook. Now, we're ordering food on an app from restaurants that specialize in delivery only. We used to shop at K-Mart, call a taxi for transport, and go to Blockbuster to rent a movie.

But guess what? The attention has shifted!

The church is not exempt from attention shifts. And the stats shared by my pastor friend prove it.

Instead of blaming our congregations for not showing up, we should ask ourselves what value we are offering to the people we're trying to reach. Are we giving people a reason to come back every week?

It's all about supply and demand. We're living in a free market enterprise. You see, the market is always right. According to our target audience, the value we're offering is only worth 1.8 Sundays of their precious time.

UNLOCKED

We need to have the courage to challenge the very thing that has been such a blessing to us for so many years.

Yet we continue to build systems and structures around the assumption that the model we used for the last fifty years is the model we're going to have until Jesus comes back. We continue to invest our time, energy, and money based on the assumption that our distribution model will remain the same.

Don't be fooled. We need to understand the shifts in attention we're going through in the church and as a society.

We need to have the courage to challenge the very thing that has been such a blessing to us for so many years. Just because something worked yesterday doesn't mean it's going to continue to work the same way. In fact, it never will. The world around us is always progressing. It's always advancing. And we had better make sure we advance with it.

In marketing we're always asked three questions:
- What is the value that I bring to an organization?
- Who can benefit most from that value?
- Where do I have the attention of those people?

As long as I can simply distribute value in the places and on platforms where I have the attention of the people whom I am trying to reach, keeping them engaged with me as a ministry or organization will be easy.

It's simple, but it's not easy!

We all like the idea of change, yet few of us like the manifestation of change. Yes, change is the only constant we can expect as we move into the future.

As leaders we need to,

1. Recognize change: We need to be able to discern and recognize when the attention of our people is shifting. Statistics like the one discussed in this article should be an indicator that we need to shift as the attention shifts.
2. Embrace change: We can't just watch the world change around us and merely be a bystander who observes others go through it. We need to fully embrace the new thing that is unfolding right in front of us.
3. Anticipate change: Just because things changed once, doesn't mean they won't change again. God will lead us into change all the time to keep moving us forward. We need to get to a point at which we start to anticipate change and expect it to come to us.
4. Become a change agent: The Bible teaches us that we're the head and not the tail. As Christian leaders, we need to be those who lead the pack—those who lead the frontlines of innovation and progress.

UNLOCKED

Attention is shifting. Change is happening. And as church and marketplace leaders we're not exempt from its repercussion.

Let me give you a biblical illustration to shed some spiritual light on the matter, as well as some practical suggestions on how to navigate shifts in attention.

There is an interesting passage in the book of Judges that talks about the rise of Deborah, the woman who became the leader of Israel at a time when the attention of the people was shifting. Deborah was the one who ended up guiding God's people through a major attention shift.

Let's read about it in Judges 5: 6-8 (NKJV):

In the days of Shamgar, son of Anath,
In the days of Jael,
The highways were deserted,
And the travelers walked along the byways.
Village life ceased, it ceased in Israel,
Until I, Deborah, arose,
Arose a mother in Israel.
They chose new gods;
Then there was war in the gates.

Before we break down this scripture let's find out who Shamgar was. Shamgar isn't a popular biblical figure we learn about in kids' church. This doesn't mean he wasn't a good guy. In fact, the Bible gives us the following account of Shamgar in Judges 3:31 (NKJV):

"After him was Shamgar the son of Anath, who killed six hundred men of the Philistines with an ox goad; and he also delivered Israel."

A DECENT DAY FOR GOD'S PEOPLE

As you can see, Shamgar was a pretty good fellow. He killed 600 Philistines with an ox goad. Quite impressive, I would say. He was also the one who delivered God's people.

All of that to say, under Shamgar's leadership, God's people experienced a season of prosperity—not much to complain about. Enemies were being killed. Israel was living in freedom.

Things were alright.

Yet even though things were decent during the days of Shamgar, things began to shift. The days of Shamgar's success created a false sense of security that everything would be like this forever. An illusion that nothing would ever change.

Yet, in the days of Shamgar, three things happened:

THE HIGHWAYS WERE DESERTED

Highways are places of attention. It's the most popular way to travel from point A to point B.
Highways represent "efficiency." They are the fastest way to get somewhere. Highways are created for attention, and when attention shifts, highways get deserted.

What once was the place to be no longer serves the same purpose it once did. It just sits there empty because the people who once showed up are no longer putting the same value on its function. They are no longer willing to trade their time for its benefit.

I used to think that if you always do what you always did, you will always get what you always got. That the same action would give us the same result indefinitely. The truth is much more complicated than that. As a matter of fact, if you always do what you always did, you will get less and less from the same efforts. As the world and culture around us are changing, our efforts become less and less effective until the places that once were highways become deserted altogether.

TRAVELERS WALKED ALONG THE BYWAYS

We need to meet people where they are at. When the highways we once had are no longer serving the community we're trying to reach, they often end up in places that are not made to get them to their destination fast. As leaders we are called to develop new highways to accommodate the people we are called to and give them a way to get to their destination in the least amount of time.

> We need to be willing to leave the old behind us, even if "the old" gave us the success that got us to where we are today.

As leaders, we need to create new opportunities for our target audience to connect with the value we have to offer as a ministry. We need to innovate and turn byways into highways as we add value to those we're called to serve.

We need to be willing to leave the old behind us, even if "the old" gave us the success that got us to where we are today.

VILLAGE LIFE CEASED

Village life talks about community. When we are unwilling to shift with the changes that are happening around us, village life will cease to exist.

Village life is the community of people you do life with. When the people you try to serve in your ministry don't experience a sense of community, it will be the beginning of the end.

How do you facilitate an environment that is conducive to village life in an ever-changing world?

Fifty years ago, village life was defined as those living within the same geographical proximity. In other words, your village consisted of those you lived close to. Your neighbors, the people down the street, the baker on the corner. In other words, your village was defined by those whom you lived close to.

Then village life shifted in the 70s and 80s when you didn't necessarily have a sense of community with those who lived on your street, but more with those you worked with, went to school with, played tennis with, etc. These people didn't necessarily live close to you, but they did life with you in other places.

Today, my fourteen-year-old son has friends he never sees in person. He relates to those he will never meet in a digital environment online. Does that make it less real? No, it doesn't. It's just different.

Village life ceases to exist if we're unable to navigate the attention shift.

BE LIKE DEBORAH

Deborah was able to navigate the attention shift. She rose up as a mother in Israel and, as implied by the context of this scripture, brought an end to the three negatives above. We need to be like Deborah and shift our efforts from doing what we've always done to figuring out where our people are at today. Meet them their needs according to where they are and offer value where they are at.

> Expect resistance when you embrace change.

Let's create new highways and reinstate true village life by embracing change and anticipating the changes of the future.

EXPECT WAR IN THE GATES

Verse 8 of Judges 6 talks about "war in the gates." Even Deborah experienced conflict. Expect resistance when you embrace change. It's part of the process. But when you do, it will be worth it in the end. Innovation will challenge status quo thinking, but will ultimately result in new paradigms and ways to serve well those we are called to serve.

CHAPTER 17

SHEPHERDS IN THE WILDERNESS

What Happens When Our Paradigms Are Stuck in the "Old Normal"?

Many of the "truths" we cling to depend greatly on our point of view.

These are great words spoken by the legendary Obi-Wan Kenobi.

As leaders, we lead others through the lens of what we perceive as truth. Our perception is our reality, and we are leading our organizations and ministries accordingly.

The challenge is that perception is not always a reflection of the truth, but more about the context of the moment in a relatively small window of time.

' # UNLOCKED

Our leadership capacity is limited to the areas where perception and truth overlap.

In his book, *The 7 Habits of Highly Effective People*, Stephen Covey said it this way: "Each of us tends to think we see things as they are, that we are objective. But this is not the case. We see the world, not as it is, but as we are—or, as we are conditioned to see it."[4]

None of us is exempt from this. We all see the world as we are conditioned to see it by our culture, our history, our upbringing, our experiences, the media, people's opinions, and so on. Our realities easily get skewed and will therefore deviate from the truth.

As a result, our leadership capacity is limited to the areas where perception and truth overlap.

As leaders we need to open ourselves for alternative realities beyond our current ones so that our perception of the world around us can be aligned to "truth" in order to lead more effectively.

The other day I was reading in the book of Numbers where it says: So they said to one another, "Let us select a leader and return to Egypt" (14:4).

Wow! Really?

---

[4] Stephen Covey, *The 7 Habits of Highly Effective People: Powerful Lessons in Personal Change* (New York, NY: Simon & Schuster, 2004), 14.

Think about this for a moment....

Here are God's people. They just escaped the horrible regime of Pharaoh in the land of Egypt where they had been stuck for hundreds of years. They are about to step into the promise that they had heard about from their ancestors for centuries. As they found themselves at a pivotal point in history, and were going to actually inherit that promise, their conclusion was that they really needed to "select a leader and return to Egypt."

Crazy, right? How stupid!

What was it that was inside them that was so powerful that it would keep them from God's promise when they were so close to inheriting it? And what do we need to learn as leaders from their mistakes that will prevent us from falling into the same trap?

As I was meditating on these questions, I concluded that their perception of the truth was the thing that kept them from all that God had in store for them.

Somehow, they had come to believe that it was better to die in Egypt than it was to die in the promised land. Something in them made them default back to the situation that had mentally conditioned them for 430 years.

The paradigm that was formed over the course of their captivity caused them to make this statement:

And all the children of Israel complained against Moses and Aaron, and the whole congregation said to them, If only we had died in the land of Egypt! Or if only we had died in this wilderness! Why has the Lord brought us to this land to fall by the sword, that our wives and children should become

victims? Would it not be better for us to return to Egypt?
—Numbers 14:2-3 (NKJV)

There were only three possible outcomes of their situation:

- Die in Egypt
- Die in the wilderness
- Die in the promised land

What a way to look at the world!

Because Egypt had conditioned their thinking for all these years, they preferred to go back to what they had known for so long, instead of the other two scenarios.

What makes us believe that we are any different?

I don't know about you. But these stories in the Bible actually freak me out. Why? Well, it's simple. These stories are not just about them. These are stories about us!

If it happened to them, it could happen to us. In fact, could it be possible that we've lived most our lives under the perception that we're leading right while in reality we're falling into the same traps that these people fell into?

The paradigms we lead through determine the outcome of our efforts. This is a scary thing when you think about it. What experiences from the past have contributed to our belief system that have made us into the leaders we are today?

Let's explore three basic leadership paradigms that I believe all affect us on some level. We've all adopted leadership styles that are, to some extent, rooted in mindsets that are produced by the following examples.

LEADING LIKE SLAVES IN EGYPT

I know what you are thinking. "That's not me!"

But let's slow down a minute before drawing that conclusion. Don't be too quick to dismiss the possibility that you share this leadership perspective.

Take a deep breath and think about it for a minute. Here are God's people—people who had a covenant, a history, and a relationship with God, just like you and me. These were His people. People He loved and people who loved Him.

In other words, they were people like you and me!

Apparently, it is possible for God's well-intentioned people to spend 430 years working their butts off to build something completely foreign to what God had in mind for them. For hundreds of years, they spent their time, energy, and effort building pyramids that belonged to a different kingdom. Not only did they not build something in line with what God had in mind; they actually produced something that fortified the enemy.

If this doesn't freak you out, then I don't know what does!

Four hundred and thirty years is a long time. Being in a situation like this for over ten generations will mess with you big time. Your perception of reality will be impacted. Your situation will become your default. In fact, as horrible as it sounds, it actually becomes your safe place.

If it happened to them, it can happen to us.

Our perception of reality has the potential to keep us from greatness!

The question we should ask ourselves is, *what are we spending our time, energy, and money on that is completely foreign to the Kingdom that God is trying to build?*

Are we building the church? Or are we merely investing our time unknowingly building pyramids because our perception of our reality has adapted to a false truth?

LEADING LIKE SHEPHERDS IN THE WILDERNESS

Another leadership paradigm to explore is the one that God's people experienced for forty years after the incident described in Numbers 14:4. God intervened and decided to send all of them back into the wilderness to die.

However, there is one short sentence in Numbers 14:33 that provides a powerful insight for us as leaders that could impact the way we lead our organizations and ministries.

Here it is: "And your sons shall be shepherds in the wilderness forty years, and bear the brunt of your infidelity, until your carcasses are consumed in the wilderness" (NKJV).

As God judged the older generation whose paradigm was still rooted is the "old normal" of Egypt, He declares a promise to the younger generation. He promises them everything He had originally promised their fathers.

There was one catch, though: they had to wait it out and spend forty years as shepherds in the wilderness. They had to be patient and wait until the older generation had passed away. Then, and only then, were they able to transition from the wilderness into what God had in mind all along.

Now take another moment and think about this.

By circumstance, not by choice, a whole generation had become something that they were never destined to be! The decisions of those who went before them caused a whole generation of leaders to be shepherds in the wilderness!

These were young kids when this all came down. Their paradigm was formed in the forty years that followed.

Think about it. When you are forced (through the decisions of others) to become something you were never supposed to be for that length of time, you simply will start to accept that the reality of the wilderness is the "normal" you're supposed to experience.

Could it be that we've been leading our ministries like shepherds in the wilderness while, in reality, there is so much more?

Is it possible that our leadership paradigm has resulted in leadership styles that actually prolong our wilderness experience rather than propelling us into all that God has for us?

I believe we owe it to ourselves (and the people we lead) to ask ourselves these questions.

LEADING LIKE OWNERS OF THE PROMISE

Our true inheritance is not found in Egypt, nor the wilderness. It is found on the other side of the River Jordan. If we are going to conquer the promises that God has for us as individuals, as well as the church collectively, it's going to require a true paradigm shift in how we lead.

> # We have to move into uncharted territory if we're going to inherit all that God has for us.

As leaders, we must be willing and able to reform the mindsets by which we lead. Progress happens on the edge of chaos. We have to move into uncharted territory if we're going to inherit all that God has for us. This demands that we think differently about how we lead and build our organizations.

In my effort to help you identify whether you're preconditioned to one or more of the leadership paradigms discussed in this chapter, I have outlined some of the characteristics for each of them.

I hope and pray that this will help you break away from what is keeping you from all that you can be:

LEADERS IN EGYPT
- All activity happens in one place
- Culture and leadership bow to external control
- Hard work fortifies the enemy

- Passive attitudes
- Lack of vision/guidance
- Enslaved to a system foreign to God's plan
- Miracles are needed, but not happening

Shepherds in the Wilderness
- Wandering activity, but around the mountain
- One-man leadership (e.g. Moses leading all)
- No work at all
- Reactive attitudes to circumstances
- Corporate vision/guidance only (e.g. following the cloud)
- Freed from slavery
- Miracles needed and happening

Owners of the Promise
- Dispersed across the land (individual inheritance)
- Empowerment to lead individually
- Hard work to fortify the Kingdom
- Proactive attitudes for success
- Personal vision for all people
- Empowered for greatness
- No miracles needed due to abundance

The mindsets of Egypt keep us in Egypt. The leadership styles designed to survive the wilderness keep us in the wilderness.

In order to break free from the limitations of yesterday, we have to adopt new realities that will result in new practices that will change the way we lead forever. This is not an easy task, but a difficult journey of trial and error that touches every aspect of our organizations and ministries that we are responsible for. Some will resist us and try to "*select a leader and return to Egypt,*" but the ultimate payoff is going to be worth it.

Instead of becoming the best mediocre us that we can possibly become, we will break away from status quo leadership and experience all that God has for us.

Let's move forward into the future with confidence while allowing God to align our perceptions with His truth.

CHAPTER 18

GENERATION NEXT

How the New Future Makes Room for the Old

I often say, "What got us to where we are can't get us to where we're going!"

As leaders, this is something important to understand. Why? Well, every generation is supposed to contribute to the process God has in mind to further His Kingdom across the earth. His Kingdom is ever-increasing. Therefore, tomorrow will look different than today. As leaders, we should be aware of this process so we can lead with progress and the future in mind.

When we understand that tomorrow will look different than today, we will lead with a less rigid mindset, allowing us to be flexible and agile enough to embrace the change the future demands.

UNLOCKED

It's important to resist pre-defining the future based on what we've learned in our lifetime.

This is especially important when we think about our succession strategy. Who is going to carry the baton after we are long gone, and how can we hand it to them effectively? As leaders, it's important to resist pre-defining the future based on what we've learned in our lifetime, but rather keep an open mind as it relates to how the next generation will lead.

Our goal can't simply be to perpetuate what we've spent our lives building by demanding the same exact thing from those we raised.

As we're thinking through our "succession plan," we must keep in mind that what the future needs is not what we were able to provide in the present. Even though we can provide the next generation with the wisdom we've accumulated over the years, we have to stay away from telling them how to do it.

Consider the following account in 2 Kings 6:1-2 (NLT):

> *One day the group of prophets came to Elisha and told him, "As you can see, this place where we meet with you is too small. Let's go down to the Jordan River, where there are plenty of logs. There we can build a new place for us to meet."*

"All right," he told them, "go ahead."
"Please come with us," someone suggested.
"I will," he said. So he went with them.
When they arrived at the Jordan, they began cutting down trees. But as one of them was cutting a tree, his ax head fell into the river. "Oh, sir!" he cried. "It was a borrowed ax!" "Where did it fall?" the man of God asked. When he showed him the place, Elisha cut a stick and threw it into the water at that spot. Then the ax head floated to the surface.

This passage demonstrates the purest form of what I believe succession should look like. A new generation of leaders raised by Elisha the prophet had concluded their current location was too small. Isn't that exactly what we're talking about? The present is too small to accommodate the future!

The sons of the prophets explained to Elisha that they felt constricted by the *status quo*. The new generation was asking permission to leave their hometown and go to a new place that they envisioned for themselves to create the future.

I'm not sure what I would have done in Elisha's situation.

There he was, having spent his life raising a generation of leaders. He trained them. He equipped them. He taught them everything they knew. And now they were complaining about how constricted and limited they felt in their current situation. They just wanted to leave the place where they had grown up. They just needed to get out. It was no longer satisfactory to them to stay where they had been their whole lives.

UNLOCKED

Surprisingly, Elisha didn't get offended. He didn't get angry. He didn't misunderstand. In fact, he discerned what was really going on and permitted them to go! He realized that if the next generation was truly going to be and do all that God had for them, he just had to let them move away from what they had known for all those years. He knew that what had always been could not be part of the future. He had to let them go.

As a result, he simply responded with a two-letter word: "Go" (v. 2).

And as Elisha permitted the next generation to go, something remarkable happened. The sons of the prophet turned around and invited Elisha to be part of the new: "Please come with us" (v. 3).

The sons didn't try to fit into the existing world, but they invited the existing world with them into the new dwelling place that they were about to create. Like the sons of the prophets, the place where we currently dwell has become too small for what we should be.

Instead of trying to fit in, we should invite the past to become part of the new future that we're supposed to create. Not to perpetuate the past in the future, but to recontextualize some of what the past has offered us as part of the future we should aim to create.

Elisha agreed and decided to leave the dwelling that he had been in all his life. He decided to move into the future by following a new generation of leaders. Yes, things were going to be different, but because Elisha recognized the season of God, he could be a blessing to that new generation.

> **Elijah disciplined himself to be flexible enough to allow the next generation to lead him into uncharted territory.**

He could have been stubborn and stayed with what had worked for him all these years. Instead, Elijah disciplined himself to be flexible enough to allow the next generation to lead him into uncharted territory. As a result, in due course, Elisha was able to share wisdom and counsel that would allow him to help the young leaders solve a challenge they were encountering as they were building their new dwelling.

> **We should invite those who raised us to be part of the new future we're creating.**

He provided valuable insight that helped them recover the ax head that had gotten lost along the way. Without the ax, the sons were at a real disadvantage as they were trying to build something new. Elisha provided wisdom to recover what they needed most to create the future.

We have to learn from this. Yes, we have no option but to pack our bags and leave our current dwellings. But in going, we should invite those who raised us to be part of the new future we're creating.

Whether you're part of the older generation or the younger generation one thing is for sure. The place where we dwell has become too small! As older leaders, let's allow the next generation to take us to new places. Let's allow them to take undeveloped land and turn it into a place we could have never imagined. As younger leaders, let's see beyond the present into a future that has yet to be created and invite those who raised us to be part of creating it.

The future is ours. The future is bright. Let's create it together!

AVAIL +

TRY FOR 30 DAYS *AND RECEIVE*
**THE SEQUENCE TO SUCCESS
BUNDLE** FREE

$79 VALUE

+ BOOK
+ STUDY GUIDE
+ ONLINE COURSE
+ LIVE CLASS
+ MORE

The Art *of* Leadership

This isn't just another leadership collective...this is the next level of networking, resources, and empowerment designed specifically for leaders like you.

Whether you're an innovator in ministry, business, or your community, **AVAIL+** is designed to take you to your next level. Each one of us needs connection. Each one of us needs practical advice. Each one of us needs inspiration. **AVAIL+** is all about equipping you, so that you can turn around and equip those you lead.

THEARTOFLEADERSHIP.COM/CHAND

THE AVAIL PODCAST
HOSTED BY VIRGIL SIERRA

www.ingramcontent.com/pod-product-compliance
Lightning Source LLC
Chambersburg PA
CBHW070540090426
42735CB00013B/3031